THE BEGINNING SPRING

The
BEGINNING SPRING

by ROBERT LOUIS NATHAN

PHILOSOPHICAL LIBRARY
New York

LIBRARY
College of St. Francis
JOLIET, ILL.

DEDICATED TO

SUSAN

Copyright, 1969, by PHILOSOPHICAL LIBRARY, INC.
15 East 40th Street, New York, New York 10016

All rights reserved

Library of Congress Catalog Card No. 75-81815

MANUFACTURED IN THE UNITED STATES OF AMERICA

901
N277

Contents

53386

Book I

WINTER

Chapter 1

THAT I AM OF ancient Hebrew lineage speaks throughout this work. This is noted to remind of the lingering potency of an age's abandoned Culture and of its Gods. All of my being is woven into this essay though I attempt to mirror only that which is apart from myself. The fading Western era and that first, sightless, breath of the coming World Culture is the reason for this effort. My being is a fact of the West's winter storm. I exist, yet the West is of the become. For this book could not be wrought unless the harvesting was finished and this now was a sterility hastily hidden. It must be said without tremor that the West is dead. And thus I issue this monograph on her dying season. The marching of Europe's peoples is ended. Victories mighty have been won. The West has propelled herself to far lands and seas but today her soul is silent as no leagues of spirit remain to be traversed. The hands vibrate still with nerve and muscle contractions as they grasp to control the direction of her motion in space and time. The mind has forgotten creativity and is computer-like, reacting to challenge with images of past responses and always ending with repetitious fantasies of impossible utopias. Never a new thought bursts thru the ever compacting ideas of the West.

Motion, space, and time are signals denoting the moment. In this final season only space persists as an essence of the Culture's reality. Movement is of art and science, of creation and sureness; time is to be aware. Space is actuality, the substance of existence. Motion and time are apparent when man is historically productive, when he is creating societies, thought, and cultures. To be aware is to be creative in the inner, the sensitive, meanings of the resurging reproduction that belongs to living matter. Awareness is the symbol of being that intuitively is in balance with life. To be aware is to be constantly associated with creative completeness. There can be no art without the sentient act of awareness. History as compilation of fact is as the plankton skeletons falling endlessly to form clay mantles on the ocean floor. Prehistory is that which was present before man learned to create Cultures. Man contributes most to awareness, to life as a creative force, when he structures Cultures. Man's early formation of environment, his classic besting of surroundings, are worthy as history because they prepared man's capability as a creator of Cultures. Man as a species of animal is old and moulded to patterns set to hardness. Cultures are youthful in time as measurement but ancient as an untapped solution deep in his interior self. A need to formulate Cultures was apparent in Man's destiny before he had earthed his first city's wall. Man as a race had a indistinct idealization of a society matured to great things. Man as animal has forged his own limitations in social and individual behavior. For he was not chained by birth to be restricted to an existence as a biologically determined organism. The wild horses of Eurasia were guided to their pasture by instinct, and man too is a wanderer. A nomad who seeks a rimmed valley only when the paths are high with the heaviest snow, Mankind searches for a social order that satisfies his needs as a soul enchanted animal.

Art is motion alive, a myriad complexity of combining symbols extended into dramatic colors and shadows. These combinations as seen by the artist are continuously in permutability, they seem to have movement distinct in themselves. The artist is aware of symbols as art because he has the essential knowledge that his milieu is alive. He must never be repentant of life except when he fails to enlarge it with his art. Life is a privilege and especially to those who are cognizant of its simplicity as reflected in regeneration and decay. Living matter that is capable of thought and images is indeed wondrous. Artists as poets, painters, sculptors, and composers should be aware of their responsibility to add to the storehouses of creativity. It is before the age of Cultures that men learned to be artists, creators of symbols that excite and inspire the inner senses. The artists of pre-Culture worked their trade as priests in expiation of the unknown but the Cultural artist gifts his handicraft in glorification of God and courage though bearded by the tragedy of being. Awareness is a sensitivity to life, a brimming passion for images in beauteous motion as restitution to the joy of existence. To be aware is to love in total capitulation to the presence of life. A poet in the ecstasy of his labour is a man whose soul trembles with the ennoblement of life's awarenesses.

A Culture is the full story of men in completion of their potential and finality. A less complex society develops into a Culture only by the willingness of diverse peoples to be alloyed into a totality of attitude and form. Cultures came after man had trained himself to be of the flocks and harvest, after he answered the needful urge to build cities. The social growth that is termed Culture is infrequently attained; however that order which is called civilization is a comparatively general society that is recognizable by its lack of incandescent spirit. Civilizations exist as the Culture's ossified form and as societies that reached not their fullest possibilities but were adept at style. A Culture realizes mankind's need of inspirational art, puissant science, and adoration of God. A civilization is a negation to these goals as it is beyond the realm of creativity.

Motion has ceased in this winter of the West. Each particle of matter is titled and organized by the technicians. Meaningless has art and science become since confidence fled the Western soul. This enervation became politically identifiable on the felling of the peasant-king Lincoln, for thereon followed the breakage of faith in democracy as utopia. The beheading of the French royalty could be assumed to be a signal flag of progress, but the murder of Lincoln could only presage disaster. A debased Christianity was replaced by socialism as the object of religious fervor and in these manners did autumn end. The fashion was to kill the kings, the Bourbons and the Lincolns. To destroy both monarchy and republicanism swiftly. Money instantly seized the crowns and ruled nakedly without the softening traditions of charity and faith as duty. The landed way, feudal and Jeffersonian, was mated to the despair of Cultural decay. Christianity as a way of life and as morality could not accept the reign of gold, but the children of Christ on earth did not remonstrate as they had exerted their Will in the periods of Cultural construction. By the mid-nineteenth century the churches had weakened their holds yet the concept of a universal brotherhood and the need for a vision greater than reality had not died. Finally socialism as the economic and political underside of transcending humanism and faith capsized Christ's churches. A desire for immediate amelioration of palpable injustices took custody of European men's hearts. Socialism became the newest nirvana, the peasant-proletariat solution for their quest of a haven from a draconian reality. By its placement in the West's history socialism symbolized the end of the regenerative Culture. Self imposed surgery began in hope of averting death by severing the spirit from the body.

The readers of these pages will note as markers set along the road that denotes time as a future after I am dust. A tomorrow shaped by the beginning spring shall be sighted in the forest glen. Yet it is sadness that the West has died and become stillness of night where only faint sounds of unanswered pleas are heard. Not a human has been stirred with the total vibrancies of Cultural creation if he is born to this century. The sweet becomings of Europe are but wind strewn thistles for a long mournful time. Where shall I open this tale? How should I, a simple and afraid fellow, spread out the tattered rolls of man's rivers? It is my lot to speak of World History's highest summit as a fallen massif torn to dirt by an angry actuality.

Who am I to dare this poemed story? Perhaps I have conquered marvelous cities as a horsed general. Somewhere and in sometime did I reduce nations at my hand's sway and take a diadem of the oldest house and charge my sons to be acclaimed kings? Could I, a writer of meager accomplishments, have made a Christ comprehensible to savages? Were the castles of Portugal and Italy struck from the brown soil to thrust majestically past the debris of the swallowed

Athenian Culture because of anything I may have pronounced?

Peasant dances and recited odes from a thousand years of images play in my musty mind. And I see dancing children with but death as companion stride onward to find the Carpenter's sepulcher. And excited motion of driving armies rip the clouds in their eagerness to smite the Paynims. Princes caught in destiny's decision add mortar to the poem that exhausts my soul. Mozart shall be ended in the tragedy that my eye envelops as shattered slices of light spin into the dark of winter. Can all the color and adventure of the West be dispatched because an insignificant provincial strikes mad tunes in his head?

Western man defied the lonely space of the infinite and attempted to bridge it. He spun a net of invisible strands to entwine the pulsating entirety of God and life. With what authority do I malign their courage with a whimpering of this now's frozen sea and sky? My reply is measure of my soul's scope and need, for I am anchored to the saga of the European age. Yes, the hill of Roland erupts from my head spouting cavalcades of sworded knights astride huge steeds. Yes there resounds in my mind's world the song of the West and it is as if my spirit is amove. Always children know that the seas muster themselves with immense grace. And farmers perceive that the growth that crumbles the earth is a replica of the Lord's beginning movement. It is apparent that life fructifies reality with being. As the coverlet sky sustains itself as immortal, so I accept the essences of the surging West into my very organs. My involvement with her welfare is so great that it would seem I must be parent to the West. Because of my love I am compelled by her stricken condition to bewail her passing. Forever I shall be of the West. Portering her courage and honour stoically to the grave and once there, with boldness acquired from the Norsemen, I shall reach down to the richness of memory and initiate a becoming from her fertility.

This shedding of sterile winter is but the Nile lying down upon the Egyptian loam. River of the season of fruit spreads her water indiscriminately, without plan, over the land until the last, high ridge contains the violence of birth. As did the Pharaohs renounce potency, so the pride of Athens was slowly surrendered to the ebbing Cultural force.

Force is the physical extension of man's Will and is profusely available in the days of Cultural blossom. Will as acted out by force produces expressions of awareness and form. Man is not spontaneously capable of edicting a Cultural spring out of its ordered time sequence. However in any moment there exist some few who cannot help but strive for a newer dawning. Destiny fills their souls with a bravery that awes the dichotomies inseparable to reality. Wills of resiliency and persistence launch forceful acts that challenge the systematic rhythm of mundanity. Seemingly chaos inspires their Will to Cultural semination. When their lodgment in history is appropriate these men are attracted to the newly born Culture in a furious arousal. They struggle not to be separate but to swim nearer and so unite with the spuming entity.

A man who is able to exhibit force in the age of winter is a being who hears the otherwise lost winds of summer. He listens to the irredeemable and for an instant the notes lead his imagination to incredible musings. In the most difficult of nights there shall be found song-teemed men who search forward desiring to be the light's tip.

Stilly quiet is the tomb of Lincoln this eve. No soldier pridefully accompanies the sky enshrining moon on its motioning above the stone encased sediment. Still are the leaves that guard his tomb, and no monarchs broach the silent mornings with retinues and crowds enthralled. All agone are Lincoln's visions and proclamations. He dueled death with a desperate dignity until emptied of life. It was his assassination that brands the last Western people as concomitant to Europe's failure. America was forever included in a wedded burial with master Europe. Yet there were the early years when the Yankee people seemed to be inducing myths of forest and plains giants that might have been progenitors of an historical incident. Decades extant when the Americans portrayed a peasant folk not dissimilar to those who usher Cultures to fruition. Today it is clear that America's role was indistinct from the Occident, but there were dusks when a dream did stimulate Columbian man to hope of a Cultural birth. This mystical belief ceased to be a major chord with the commencement of the Civil War, for at its conclusion America capitulated to the phantom of progress and became mercantile, industrialized, and moneyed. A half century followed when the farming class had an undefined faith in themselves and their land but this milky dream was not communicated to the children.

I adore the West as deeply as the holy hermit who in his desert cave attempts communion with beloved God. As I am born to the finality of the West I am compelled again to envision the entire looming so as to comprehend this present waste land. Words as Vienna, Athens, Memphis, are fragrant with buddings. All were cities born of brawling, landed peoples who demanded impossible goals for themselves. And in accomplishing the unfeasible they also corroded in the abrasive that is time as age.

Chapter 2

THE GERMAN is the archetype Western man. From the plains and meads of the Frankish domains the West's matrix was cleaved. Spengler is rightfully abused for his nationalism and deification of his fatherland's finer individuals. The zealot's passion for nation is a disease infectious to any man of this depraved season. Spengler's gift is of soul and spirit and not of iron or blood. He is the world's first Cultural historian, admittedly narrow in faith and hope but marvelous with historical instinct and intuitive perceptions. Polybius pounds his hand to lectern and declares that he teaches the history of his world and that thee should be educated by his observations. Spengler shows an empathy for the flowings and the morphology of Cultures and their successor civilizations. He tutors not fact but awareness of history as motion and time, as if history was a soaring glider of music. To be a historian as this fellow was, one must be sensitive in relation to the present as compared to dissimilar ages. To envision the dissonant and the compatible as one portrait of the Culture.

I long to be a poet, a man who loves and yet mourns each instant of living and expresses his impressions in word images. My soul engulfs my reality with its love of awareness. Early I sensed the earth passing beneath the counterpoised sky. My longing is to love in each moment of my experience and this is only heightened by the admission of death. For death and I are not strangers, my season bellows with the shrieking dying and in acknowledgement of its supremacy I cherish every gentle touch I may take. I come not to surpass any man's artistic or scientific masterwork but rather to declare the essential beauty visible in any season. To give hope unchained in man's dreams is my voyage, it is the very reason for my love and existence. I refute those winter men who seem not aware of the fleeting sea of history, of dying peoples, ideas, and Cultures, and of birth, of a fertility magical with hopeful love. Never shall I claim title savant for my nature is of a warrior's soul metered by a poet's sensitivity. Give me and my labour no name, only say that I struggle to vent newer methods of viewing history.

Years is a word that should be only heard in the singular. Year is the sound of the sea breaking over the shore shallows and spraying free the mud of earth. The sea, sea, listen to the word as it comes from the tongue and is propelled into the become of the inner lip. Wisdom is birthed when the spirit of the boy lives in the old man's body. When the boy's soul fills the corporeal until the aged flesh is spring thirsting with life to bear. Years is but a dreadful sound and can not represent the living blood spent. Years are knots looped on a frayed thread that spells out death. A man should have no pinpricks as demarcations in time, for he is a single strand of past history. A band that has no direction in space and is not measurable by universal time, but only by incautious symbols. The recording of years is the mechanical expression of grief, of the inaction of dying. Cultural history as gauged by solar time is a vision engendered by man's peculiar spatial inflection and is most pertinent to the sowing of fields and the observance of holy days. Mankind is separated from time as a lever is to actuality, for we are a condition to life subject to decay.

Trees are of men for they are allegoric of a fecund luster and are discernible in the organic act of generation and decay. In walking a forest the couplet of creation and decay is silhouetted, for at the same footstep there is the fallen, insect gutted, remainings of a once leaf shielded oak. In the cooled space provided by the rot veined log one may see the slight sprig that shall be the tree boisterous. And the dead and the alive plant are one symmetry, one organization of time. No registration of time as future is traceable. Decay is fact, but new life is spontaneous and unrecognizable except as related to the recording of the definable past. Time is the span between space and matter on which movement is the catalyst. God and time are one thought and are a containment of actuality that is incomprehensible even to those of strict dedication. God exists as time, He is presentable as light and motion but no instrument can verify his being. The technician of winter trusts the velocity of molecular action while the poet of any age believes in the light. A man may reveal time to himself as does the child who watches the motionless eternity of sky entertained by the ballooning clouds. To a man of hope time becomes not cruel but as real as love and despair, as prevalent as history, and fertile in promise of life.

The sea gathers herself in the shifting silt of the bottom and in a ponderous heaving rises to sway the earth. Moon bold, silver bastard, half planet, is but a shinny bauble to be held fast by the cresting waves. Frozen or blood warm the sea nurtures the planet and yields life to the become. I am a dreamer, an unpolished vessel that desires the power of the sea in my writings but I am conscious of my inadequacy, my failure to compare.

Empty my clutching, damp, hands rake at the void that is my Culture's death. My freedom filled soul, my quickly ignited mind are futile gifts if cast into the widening orifice of the West's disintegration. I must control my thoughts and hurtle them to future becomings. Time and sea are my friends, sharing their energy to inspire my hopes. As a novitiate fisherman I plead that the sea remember all that was man's past and convey once again that which is alive to the land.

Balm is needed to ease the aching wounds of life dying. A becoming is desired, for it is the season of flower. With the fulfilment the hunter who once ran the chase has become a provider who plans a trap to catch his prey. Young moments are never wasted except by dying. To speak in a peal of rhythmic prose is my constant intention since first I wished to paint music with words. My charge is to prepare my visions with the skill that they deserve and not to suffocate introspections with wordiness and arrant presumption. Sad it is, for I have no streams of faultless rhyme and yet I might consider myself an apprentice poet if I could strain one canvas of poetry imbued with the instant when the running sea of night is stroked by the fingertips of dawn. To have the power to call the tides, to unfurl their waves into motion, is my craftsman's hope. To arrange words in such a meticulous frame that they explode brilliantly across the virgin whiteness. Printed fables that parade in profusion before my best eye that is set deep behind my mask. I shall be an artist always for when a lad I was stolen by the sun's glow and the night's gleam.

The dark is a word sound for fear. Death is not synonymous with dark but it is a point that persists in the spaces where light is damned. Darkness is the sea of one's travails thru the vapors of fear. Man himself is a sentient ship that imprints the hidden ocean with efforts to exhume the inexplicable. If man had not iridescent dreamings to delineate his walk in the dark of sleep, he would refuse to escape the awake.

Facts are not urgent to this presentation for it is thought and music that glue this work. Statistical percentiles are excluded from this book as are technical equations, for the curved designs of man's imagination are my cutting tools. I attempt to bid spirits from the earth's entrails and they appear only on mystical incantation. My magic is the art of the West. A few notes of Mozart cannonade away all the factualizations of this disturbed century. Today the totalitarians rule, and they manipulate men's souls for the basest of motives. The castaways of the autumn facade lead this end season to its dispatch. Not one of the stenciled Caesars promulgates the essential call for courage that our age yearns to hear. To whisper justly, without histrionics, that to fight the winter fury with devoted Will might preserve man's integrity.

Spengler was mistaken for Cultures do pass to each other particular material. Usually it is that which has to do with the fact of technology, but rarely and unbeknownst a cell of soul is given to the stranger. Lingering strophes from the Peloponnesia do bend the ragged branches of the West's winter. What is irrefutable is Spengler's theory of Cultural morphology. This is an achievement of the highest artistic creation. *The Decline of the West* must not be read as diatribe or as a didactic lecture, rather it must be interpreted as the lover of Bach listens to the music sounding in his inner world. The *Decline* is poetry, in effect, as is Dante's *Inferno* or Milton's *Paradise Lost,* but this twentieth century poem finds the journey ended with the splendid marches to Heaven and Hell long consummated. This last age of the West is a purgatory between life and death. Today the simplest men may be distorted and made insane by the psychic terror that our reality inflicts on them.

No Culture has reached higher than has the West and none shall have a fall so bitter. Nothing in nature or time approaches the West's capacity to inflict damage to herself. Madness is the plague of this season. In former centuries streets may well have been depositories for excrement and refuse with rivers bloated with corpses, but in those ages the soul's attitude toward life was not diseased. In this today man's sanctity is corrupted and the glorious West passes from the stage on the howlings of her demented peoples.

Chapter 3

A SHIP, MASTS three towering high, makes merry with the running sea. Sails are whitened except where mottled by the bow sprinted waves. All awhite except where grey aged and stressed. Gleaming folds move in imitation of wind, all white but where yellowed by a thousand months sailing below the sun hostaged skies of the multitudinous waters. The ship is captivating in aspect, handsomely groomed when in roust with a northern storm. In those moments when smallish sailing craft caraveled the salted oceans the West was greatness uninhibited. The wooden boats etched the West's determination to command space near and afar. These early, resolute, ships of Europe search yonder for sunlight, for the ransom of the hunter's freedom never to be of the ploughing soil. The sailing men of Europe knew no hyper-nationalism for they were subjects of divine kings or citizens of city states. Venetians thwarted Turkish expansion on the placid Mediterranean while their spiritual brothers in the Hanseatic League knitted the Baltic cities into a consortium of trade and communication. From nascent Spain and coastal strip Portugal the sturdy, poop decked, vessels sailed out into stranger seas. With the Cross of Christ above their bows and a lust to possess gold in their loins, the sailors of Europe stoked the fate of the world. Perhaps the instant had arrived for stimulation and germination but without the interior Will of European man as surging energy destiny may well have been aborted.

The dream holds steady course yet it be an ice manacled ocean that echoes today's tune. To be with Nelson at Trafalgar, to be on Victory's splinter ripped gun deck with darkness combing the east while the surviving allied fleet, penned black against the failing light, is swept onto a lee shore. To sign on with Howe and fight the Revolution's dogs on the First of June. What it would have been to have sailed with Magellan and prowed the roaring fifties, to arrive and inject the existence of Europe into the Pacific. To have been a sailing man on any good ship of the line with a just master to serve with, or to captain a prowling frigate off the Antilles. Where have they gone, those ships of sail that thrusted outward until the world had been subdued and made fief to the West?

To have had a cramped birth in the least ventilated, sea washed, forecastle of a well founded sailer would have sufficed. Pneumonia, tuberculosis, and scurvy notwithstanding, for the ocean hammers linked mailed constitutions into those who survived her inaugural buffets. I have been born too late in my Culture's life to have climbed a wave lapped mast up to the flaring mainsheet cumbersome with chilling rain. Melville has writ my ode and sailed my ships and I am but a rememberer of what a fast sailer might have been. The nimble, wind chased, clippers lay as long lengths of shaling timbers below a hundred fathoms of dense salt water. The sea fills my marrow with yearning for though I am a provincial, a son of a trade's family, as a youth I desired to sail upon the oceans of earth. To wage battle with the Frenchman and to landfall unknown isles and harbours. As a child I wished to sail the oceans, to pulley the yards to adventure and be appraised by danger. Doomed are such simple wants when embroiled in the actuality of coping with Cultural disintegration.

The sailing ships of Europe were the manifestation of Western probing. A ship is the symbol of the West's ethos and is comparable to the Vandyked brown of the European plains. Geography has much to do if a people is to be great or small. The central slope of Europe curving northward above the Pyrenees and Alps was conducive to the wombing of the West. Savages of Teutonic gene angrily swarmed southward to take the bastions of the middle sea. And the lands of old Europe stood before the northern barbarians as a magical world. The hardiness of the hunter traditionally bred to warriorship is kept intact by the conditions due the life of the herdsman and peasant. Swiftly the thickly clumped woods were felled as the savage changed to become a tiller of the land. Both king and serf are dependent on the soil for their security and placement beneath the judging heavens.

Turmoil and destruction came to the Rome of the Caesars. The provinces had been long neglected and left abdicated by the city. In the souls of the slave, Christ was given comfort and entry onto the altar of the Empire. Spain, Gaul, Italy, Illyricum, are captured by the Goth, Visigoth, and Vandal. They breed with the reduced stocks of antiquity; Celt, Phoenician, Grecian, Etruscan, and Latin. In this method a thin cord of the Classical World is needled into the capes of Western man. A coloration from the Athenian Culture is apparent in the decor of the West. This is minor to the fact that the Church of Christ was sculptured by the style and passion of the dying Athenian vision of Hebrew redemption. From the hollow of late Rome, the Cross of Christ represented hope to mankind. Yet it is only because the Greek World as parvenued by Rome did collapse that a Christ was able to be. His becoming and His manner of revealment were not of fortune's chance but the gear shifting of historical necessity. Fate is impossible and erratic but history can be observed as inevitable thru the awareness of life as subject to patterns of growth and decay. Christ had to be, but what was not absolute was his ordainship and the condition of men after his coming. Jesus might have been a failure, rather man may have failed Him. It is His Church that revives from the sun choking dust of the prostrated Classical Culture to tend the babe that was the New Age. I refuse Christ as the Son of God but as a representative of the Lord He surely was, for men were instructed by His very Substance. That the Church of Europe is opposed in attitude to the original Church of Christ is understandable if examined through the lens of Cultural morphology. The Greek and Western Cultures are separate creations but in the sequence of the one dying and the other being born, a relationship of total entity is mistaken. Death, never half measured, silenced the Empire and the groping spring of

Europe in a matter of five or six centuries rapidly appeared in the lands that moribund antiquity had called home.

A false belief was assumed that the Savior had also redeemed the World as He had offered a saving to the souls of men. But there was not a Cultural redemption for a birth singular had sprung from the same valleys of Gaul and Germany. Christianity was nurtured by the Semites of the Greek winter. Jewish colonies, Hellenized in the methods of thought and free Will, disbursed about the Empire, clung to their messianic redemptive faith and thus formed the initial congregations and pulpits of Christianity. But with the removal of tolerant Arianism, the final pragmatism of matured paganistic logic, the Church became indigenous and less international. It is this contraction of vision that led to the faith that allowed the Church to become the West's edifice. The Church of Rome is but the descendant of Christ and it is this alien Church that becomes the protector of the West. A Church incapable of birth, still she is of the earth and usually has been a gentle gardener in a brutish reality. She gave water to the West's beginnings and weeded out lesser foliage.

Journey with me to the awakening of the European Culture. All of Greece is dead, nothing is intact. The crumpled structures desolate with plants of life tearing apart the colored paled walls. Homer's Gods lay broken and buried beneath the earth, blackened with flame and sworded into fragments. Spain, the plantation of Rome, is deserted, lonely. Gaul is a thousand hamlets with ten thousand jealousies. The German tribes are amove, migrating, yet slower now. Britain is a forgotten place, thing, island in the mildewed records of the once Empire. Africa and Mauretania wait as displaced granaries of Rome, fertile and industrious but a weariness barks at their ankles as indeed her peoples practice the baring of their necks for Allah's sword. Syria and Egypt are peoples no more, their histories truncated and impoverished to unanswered fantasies as the Arabians, still unnamed, are impatient at Mecca. A city state alertly exists on the Hellespont, on the stones of Megara's Byzantium. This hoary polis witnessed all that was Greece and Rome and now as Constantinople she struggles a destiny lost for a continuation of virility. This mightiest city of Asia is the inviolate remnant of Greece's form. She guards the monuments of her father's well and transmits to the invading savages from young Europe the awarenesses that the Doric warrior and Ionic seafarer had discovered. In this manner the memories of Greece are never quite hushed.

Athenian streets are rubbled with the collapse of the anatomy of a once incredibly spirited vision of existence. Lacedaemon is mentioned never but in time sealed manuscripts. Exquisite were the temples of Delphi but the vale is unshielded to the ravages of time's wind. A vast number of carnal violations have been consummated and the races of Greece have been breeded into oblivion. All of Caesar's burial robes are indistinguishable ash and stolid Pompey has been murdered on Egypt's shore, an epoch squandered. Syracuse, where Athens perished but did not die, is a rustic place where the bounding deer come to suck the stream's portion. Winter's Pompey is the last fog of Athens in Rome. Today he is ignored for he had not a springtime Homer to myth him a giant's requiem or a summer Aeschylus to mask his futile legend with tragedy's disaster. Caesar's tears are not pretended as he views the severed head. He weeps, unknowingly, not for the unsightly removal of his competitor but at the finish of the Athenian melody. End is apparent in the oracle's flame, the future is but the past of the past and Ajax is dead by another hand besides his own.

The civilization of the Classical Culture is enlarged in the volumes of World History by Julius Caesar. He is a new type king, for no empire before him has been seized or led by a man more a demagogue than less a warrior. Caesar is spoked into the dictatorship of the empire by the diastole stroke of a changing Cultural season. To compare one Culture's matching season's duration and condition to another must find highly varied resultants. A season's condition of society is a mixture of causal effect and individual creation and differs exotically from Culture to Culture. However, the rigours of Cultural morphology, the growth, decay, and death of the entity to its season does not change. That Roman civilization is sustained for several centuries beyond the demise of her parent Culture has no specific answers to the West's extremity.

Caesars do appear in the winter, or civilization season, but their power and importance to the total is a matter predicated by the character of the sole Culture. Caesarism is a technique of popular demagogy that has no connection except in outward appurtenant to the earlier aristocratic absolutism of the city states. Ulysses' world has a longish moment of death, somewhat graceful but it is Homer's age that finds this route and there is no promise that our Culture may. What is of pertinence to those who foe their Culture's end is its longevity for even a mine slave wishes to live to his allotted hour.

Caesar became Caesar because Athens is a tawdry provincial town and the becoming is forever still. His foresight repudiates the theory that only Western man is concerned with the direction of the future through actions taken in the present. Yet his dreams became dross among the waste of Cultural exhaustion. Emperors who follow do engineer monumental edifices of self-glorification as adornment of their moment, but affect grave markers, not sign posts. Julius scribed his own history and needed not a facile Josephus to enhance events and deeds. He remembered that of the past which was noble, and though he failed, he tried to respect the dissipated republic. He was born to winter but he attests the summer and autumn ghosts. Julius was the last Roman to have strength of Will to dare change.

Attica is a refrain from a breathless flute and no more mother to Heroes for with each ploughing the earth is of less generous breast. Those who guided the spasmodic and palpitating Roman Empire into a retrenching were titled fool and stranger. A robust race of warriors who had flung Xerxes backward into Asia are now represented by a city's gargantuan mob that knows not to pay the Gods a simple homage. Those few who are inseparable from warriorhood, no matter the season, battle to stay the Empire's disintegration. And all of these without exception are seduced outlanders whose unfettered tribesmen assassinate Rome, as indeed they attempt to wrap flimsy bandages around her stumps. Land is offered to slaves in hopes of increase for the demographic disaster is at last obvious. The extraordinary cities about the Roman sea become disorganized, then disordered and emptied as indeed those sand deluged cities where Xenophon encamped in the *Anabasis*. Dust settles to cover the walks and agoras, quickly the buildings are reclaimed by the drifts that seed bush to infold the disrepaired walls. Imperial trade is restricted to the environs of Constantinople for Italy is slack and sick in her bowels. German nomads carnival in streets and squares dedicated by the Vestal Virgins an age removed. Barbaric custom rules in Roman cloak and this clown's masquerade ends the Athenian adventure. As immense as the Greek was once as a creator of World History he is now devoid of the basic energy of reproduction. Uninspiring Byzantine tortuously outlives her Culture's disappearance as a house of trophies.

The years that lay despondent between the West and Athens serve as an age of incubation. It is in these days that chieftains halt their wandering clans and command them to labour in cultivation of the land. These are peoples new to history but they do flourish until they number as nations. And kingdoms are issued by these barbarians who had recently slain Athens and Rome. Barbarians unlike the docile, domesticated, Goths of the old marchlands for these were savages violent in normal intercourse. The Germans, soon to be called Franks, slaughter the crippled peoples of the prostrate Empire. Albion is plucked by Saxons grateful to leave their swampy Rhenish delta hovels. Greece is devastated of Athenian and Spartan pneuma by Ostrogoth and Visigoth who also occupy Italy and the Iberian lands. Four hundred Easters empty into the cauldron that is incipient Europe until when all seems settled the Vikings overthrow stability in a rage. Cascading spewings of aimless peoples again fill European roads forgiving the loss of past contentment in the excitement and difficulty of birth. Pillars are quarried from earth stricken pagan temples to be cut into stone for towers and nave of castle and church.

Spengler, in delineating the Classical ethos by art analysis, predicts Greek statuary as the primary symbol expressive of the Athenian spirit. He reads a dialogue of constricted time and space in the sightless eyes of the marbled men, where I divine a quest for immortality by an absence of the awareness of transitory time. Space is carved unescaping in the gold and ivory serenity of the giantess Athena, there is little sophistry in the youthful stone faces of the Greek World. A smiled lip becomes pensive only when spring is now summer and cognizant of the coming autumn.

Upholding the roof of Olynbus are the Doric and Ionic pillars that in a rare loveliness vignette the vinicultured hills off Aegaleus. Pillars that speak of the essence of Greece to her Gods. A concept of time straining to remould and flying skyward the reality of life. Time is pictured in the stone columns as perpendicular to earth and not a pathing that reaches for the become and the becoming in the same goblet of existence. To see the lengthening stoned posts seek the vermillioned black earth at dusk is to envision an expectation of immortality as automatic and demonstrative.

The sequoia does die and thunder to soil after the final infinitesimal upward surging. After death she may stand upright but the moment of crashing will be of the same as of the dying though it be delayed a score of years. Cultures must die, none exists past the dispensement of their harvesting fulfillments. As the autumnal episode is finished the spirit and need of expansion contracts in a rush. Summer ripeness is summited by a bronze anthem of boastfulness and then in the floating to rest of a page all is gone except a statement of form as the frost of winter. Prodigious empires leer in the throttled twilight in meaningless amorphism. A mechanical expression of force replaces power and confidence. The descent from the harvesting may be slightly angled or precipitous but it is absolute that the decline shall increase in severity as the number of days are summed.

There are but six Cultures in the past of man: European, Arabian, Athenian, Chinese, Hindu, and Egyptian-Mesopotamian. Each had the virtue of resiliency and persistence, Wills that contested death until the leam of dawn softened the night's horror. A passion for life and justice in art vindicates a Culture's colossal human expenditures in her rejections of defeat and failure. The totality of man's creative energy, a Culture does admit an admiration for mankind. The construction termed Culture exhibits an honour and dignity not obvious in lesser orders. A Culture is a hope of harmony versus reality, his synthesis of social redemption. Verily the first Culture of man was the River and it weathered the nailed scoring of history with a fierce Will. Ages exist and die, yet the world of the Nile does not collapse under the desiccating heat. Vast deserts, bleakly dangerous, and a fine sea separate the verdant river valley from leisurely proximity to secondary states but Egypt scatters her techniques and tautologies yet even to Ionic shore. The River Culture exists as a political power well past her demise as a creator and she is able to repel ceaseless incursions.

Chapter 4

HITLER, THOUGH in a continuous state of feminine hysteria, did possess an intuition into the less abstracted concepts of World History. From the frigid winter soil Hitler spawned, as do the twisted high mountain scrubs, who perhaps in anthropomorphic self-despisement, fantasy themselves as mighty pines that arouse myth and poetry. This totalitarian did crawl to sufficient height that allowed his frenetic thoughts to be broadcast throughout the planet. Those four decades from 1905 to 1945 glared with the brutalest of carnage that Western man has yet faced. Virulent and abhorrent days that left the Western Age stripped of foliage and prepared for the woodman's blow. An oak that had boasted buds named Michelangelo and Leonardo now produced blotched yellow halfgrowths that died abruptly beneath the burning star of earth. And it is in this iniquitous period that the cruel tyrants of the West belch forward with a wolf's foulness. Chaos came to Europe; Italy, Germany, Russia, France, Spain, and Austria were destroyed in the Forty Year War. These nations were the matter and the poetry of the West. To be sure, states with these titles were extant, but the spirit of the Culture had died. Dictators from the disappointed and abused lower classes were aided to power by the haplessly fearing ruling families. Rampant anarchy threatened Europe and men were terrified of disorder and thusly the dictators were adulated as saviors which but accentuates the current falsity. Totalitarianism is dissimilar in cause and effect from the office of dictator in the Greek city as corroborated by Plutarch, or indeed, by Livy's description of the bucolic Rome. For the dictator of the polis was chosen from the citizen peerage in specific reply to danger from hostile cities. If the men were corrupted by their position, it was an individual problem and not a symptom of Cultural decline. Sulla's amazing voluntary resignation from his position as dictator of the early Roman Empire shows the allegiance men still had to the Greek idealizations of earlier Cultural fruition.

Desperation had confused the leadership class of Europe. Sea walled England withstood the initial onslaught of the disease but was soon claimed by its fever. New Europe, the Americas, remained intact economically and politically but her attitude's direction had become hesitant as if historical withdrawal seemed a better choice than involvement.

Hitler was indicative of this time's bestiality. He was a German of pure tribal blood but his soul was crippled villainous by the age and by his own inherent weaknesses. Hitler did sense historical flow yet he was a hater of all that was simple including Christ and commiserating love. He was a European who heard the quaking cellar beams of his house. In a macabre and histrionic style he foretold the damnation of the West and did attempt to brew from the contemporary German state a restoration Empire, as his violent mind construed it. When his warrings met failure he then contrived to destroy European man, including the German people. And in this he did hasten the end.

The tyrant's hatred for the Jew was instinctive to his convulsed spirit and Hitler but represented millions of twentieth century Europeans. Seeing his own Austrian nation enter into a depressed and passive condition at the close of the nineteenth century's Cultural harvest, he was appalled to see the only recently aggressive Jew successfully contend with the compressing but abundant materialistic epoch. The Jew came late to the Western Culture as a participant, although he had been a witness for the entire millennium. Freed from their subsocial, interlocked, habits and hyperorthodoxy they came to the feast with a great hunger, as if in a ravenous state from an overlong sleep. In comparative ease they began to dominate the debates of late autumn and winter. Hebrews unleashed from their ghettos by the Napoleonic wars sprinted with the boldness of the reborn thru the closing scenes of the European Culture. Perhaps somewhat

LIBRARY
5-33 86 College of St. Francis
JOLIET, ILL.

clumsy appearing to the now sophisticated Europe in their newly won vigour, they struck thoughtful and idealistic sparks that fought the darkness.

Hitler was inflamed with a maddening hate as he watched this swordless, landless, strangely circumcised Jew attach himself with gusto to the Faustian image, while he failed to realize his own personal dream of being a functioning artist. Even the queerly clothed Jew may be affected by the story of Christ and the lines of Shakespeare. And he may wordlessly revere those very institutions that have so cravenly maltreated him, knowing that they also acted as guardian to his Culture, which was the same West. For the Jew of Europe belonged tissue and nerve to the Culture and he was as committed to it as he was to his own God. Without admitting the oneness of the West and Christ, the Jew accepted their sameness and respected their mutual agonies for he shared this actuality intimately. The Jew was feared by Hitler, as he correctly understands that they have made a successful transmutation from a subcultural legacy into the protagonist's role of the Declining West. The outcast Jew brought a discipline of mind and sureness of soul to the West just as those qualities began to be desperately needed. The European Jew belongs to the peoples of the West.

The science of this dying world is but a broken gate blowing unsecured in the gale of unrelenting time. As powerful as the atom may be, it has no soul that can generate adventure. This winter is cursed with technical acclamations but the materials produced by a highly adroit tool making society are abysmally unsuited in dealing with Cultural morphology. Today fantastic machines command but these instruments at our disposal have little consequence if man has not faith in tomorrow and hope of cleansing love. Science is not of exiguous complexities, not of amusement devices, not of technology teased to deliver greater stimulations to an already overgratified winter man. Each added moment into the cyclones of night reveals newer machines poised for seduction. Techniques act as blinders to reality, hiding evidence of decay from man's sight.

True science is creation equal to that of art, and far into

the autumn years the West produced scientific thought unsurpassed in previous ages. However by this funeral century only manual dexterity remained, as scientific insights became blunted by Cultural instability. Mechanics are applied to all endeavors no matter how significant to spirit.

This season has gifted only one worthy reward to men in the field of technical skill, the prolongation of the life term. The lifting of death but one brief glance is an incontestable achievement. To have this accomplished in the midst of howling corruption is hopeful. Let it be known that while European man slew millions of his own sons, while he implanted cancers in pregnant females, while extruding efficient death contrivances, while evil garroted pity, let it be chanted in the long corridors of the asylums that he loved life with a peasant's devotion. And with this love he was inspired to cure the pestilences. The miraculous remedies were composed in the late autumn and winter, thus again establishing that spiritual motivation can exist in seasons of brutality.

Man lifted his hands skyward in supplication and begged God's forgiveness. Man said to the Lord that the young men despaired of the future. Man spoke to the Lord and said that they were informed that everything may be lost. They praised the Lord as magnanimous and pleaded for mercy. They told Him they knew their souls were selfish and malicious but also that they were content with His love, and did love Him, and did love their brothers sometimes. And because of this emotion they had cured the diseased, many blind and dumb, and a few sad children. God heard and decided not to loosen the world into a forever abyss.

The seventh Culture shall be to history as the oceans to fish and man. It shall be an age of change and drama, yet the soul of the dead West will be free and Handel's oratorios will be sung again. The seventh world of earth shall hold an inquiry into the European ode. Columbus will again chart a grassed sea as shall William of Normandy once more be necklaced with his relics of saint bones as he rides out to the beckoning lines of the arching universe. The massive conflicts of the West will be studied minutely for causal effects. This Culture shall be named in a candid simplicity, Earth. Open decked craft with spread sail, captained by very ancient Gods, shall veer their prow's aim to revisit the new, brighter Earth.

The West has twirled the moments old so that a slowly swinging gown has shyly lifted to cradle the land from light. No more shall the sky hear the triumphant shout of the West as it conquers the unsearched.

Book II

BRIGHT ATTICA

Chapter 1

BOY WITH SHARPENED SWORD of wood rushes forward to battle giants and Hydras. Boy with slicing stick plays under air whitened sun, his hair light and blown, eyes rounded with animation. The child grows hardy under the roof of the inner sea. Youth on Attica plain dreams of Argo and thinks himself a Hero to be.

To stand on rock promontory above the agitated waves with worn bronze hilt in hand and boast to Poseidon that life is a regal adventure is to be a Greek.

He and the Westerner share in the goals of life if not in attitudes toward it. Both were nurtured in the warrior's creed of daring and boldness. Each came from societies where swordsmen were more than protectors or soldiers of property. It was the audacious vitality of the aggressive war leader that activated the need for walled cities. And the city is not a city until it is walled apart from the turned over fields. The warrior is tempered by the maturing society into the aristocrat who directs, as coincidental to his demand for an interesting and stimulating world, traditional superstitions into innovative form and art. Little unrest mars the early Culture, as physical oppression is not needed to constrain the slave and serf. Sparta's treatment of the Helots marks herself exception, not in spirit to the entirety of Greece, but obstinate in form, as seen in her lack of defensive walls. Her impervious structure is the discipline and staunchness of her war trained nobility. To the Greek warrior, Spartan soldier or Athenian sailor, death and wound are the badges of resolution and breasting spirit and not of avarice or conceit. Warriorhood is of prideful deed as was it not the warrior who sired the kings and they raised the cities of Cultural foment.

The toiler of the difficult soil, the hoe man of hot fields, is the clay of the warrior. The earth labourer supports the great nobles and only by his diligent effort do they flourish. To make war is ugly; torn bellies, empty sandals, wet red sockets, all are devastating to the mind's idealizations. To slay is horrendous but as reality it does change tomorrow's nature, for good or evil. Swords are levers of spacial largess. To maim and to kill are not the traits of the civilized but all men are capable of such things to some degree, even poets and saints. Man is concerned with dichotomies, as it is the external stresses that bring forth an unbending Will. Warrior and artist are results of conscious acts of Will. Both have awarenesses of life as challenge and tragedy. One is not of animal passion and the other of gentleness for they are man and have parts intermingled. To deny either aggression or love blunts the being in the conducting of his individual totality.

It is in the age of the become that the warrior is degraded. Winter armies are the provinces of technicians and manipulators distant from actual battle. The warrior is detested by the soulless men of the become for a man bred to courage is a reminder of spring. A figure of the becoming that has died and now is to be ridiculed. In the preludes of Cultures the freeborn males were prepared to be valorous and skilled in combat, but today such fidelity to animal qualities is despised and found embarrassing. Western warriorhood as a code of life is extinct and now armies are led by mathematicians and logistical experts. Intrepidity is left to those uninitiated to contemporary weaponry and to the young who know not the meaning of sophism.

Cultures are heralded by warrior peoples. Greece began her chorus after the Dorian savages entered the lands of the shore peoples and hacked away the surface film of Minoan civilization. Without the warrior all abstractions of a healthy social apparatus are impossible. Man was separated from the animalistic environment when the spirit to be a hunter replaced that of the forager and pack acceptances. A newly forged hunter was indistinguishable from the pack. His arms and legs were crusted with caked filth and mud but inwardly a sense of boldness had begun to confront the ways of submission. He dared to stand upright even in the revealing daylight. Tenaciously gripping his stone missile he learned to bellow his new defiance at the sacred hills. The hunter, naked and perhaps wordless, commits mankind's first action in liberation. For it is he who begins the eternal gulf between himself and the other beasts. If man is creative and aware in the Age of Cultures, it is because the hunter with his cruel disregard of pain and death tore man apart from his role as a scavenger of rotted fruit and carrion.

Sky opened temples are first fashioned in patches cleared by warrior cults. Man if not a hunter still would sit on forest bogs with his ape brethren gorging on a storm's harvest of fallen pear. The act of hunting represents the original freedom for man.

The West is exhausted, the warrior has been vanquished from the seats of honour and is fallen to places of ignominious anathematization. Winter man has disobeyed God by condemning the greater animal's extinction. The horse, the elephant, and the whale are reduced to the unicorn's rarity. Today's seekers of game lurch after false mountings and tokens as if self-acceptance shall be found in these frantic pursuits.

European man has lost his need of adventure and his zest for the hunt. He no longer indulges in the chase, as he is vehicled to his weary prey. Nowhere can be found the European princely boy who races the hare with his whistling pebble. And the hunters never more circle the enraged bruin with fire hardened spears of wood. Wondrously huge but supple whale is devastated by chemical dart and Ahab is avenged a thousand fold. Man is fatigued by hardship and struggle, his perseverance has gone to fat. Thrusting Europe is motionless and she surrenders her Will to life in an hour of boredom. Will is the rearing torrent of water to the mill wheel of World History. Will is man's single essential tool. The West's final quest is if she contains sufficient Will to restrain the madness of her death throes. Shall the West leave earth alive to create the seventh Culture of man?

Short was the West's moment, emblazoned with greatness

but impaired by the calendar of her ejaculated energy. A few centuries and a thousand years from vital beginning to the dullness of senility. European man has extended his potential and now is spent to a steel clad straw man standing erect only because of the depth that his historical structure has impressed into the soil. He totters carelessly in this today and shall soon speed unto the harsh rocks.

All of this considered formally without fictitious dreams, it is admitted that I have not acquired the knowledge to spake this work. I quake in my ego at my own audacity. Who am I that trifle to scythe the winter's wheat and sweep in unhurried design the new seed to earth? A poor fool without the dimmest lamp to guide me thru the morass of my own unsureness. Making efforts to lead from the past of this day forward to that which shall be a better age is the pretentious duty I thrust upon myself. And I have never hunted and shall never be a king or a warrior. No stripped battle won armor is to be my lootings. How ill-equipped am I to throw a lengthy shadow and to enter the lists as a member of the West's destiny.

The lonely wooded bowers are never more, the brooks of freshness are sickly with daily influx of bowel evacuations in the millions. The necropolis is queen for even the oceans are contaminated by mankind's personal and industrial refuse. And thus, the once creating city is empty of poets and kings. Christ who knows not how to forget love is despoiled and unattended in the bleak, polluted, cities. Forest crowned hillets are truncated to make room for the ribboning tracts of hovel dwellings that postulate throughout the world's urban intestines. Only the sea stays the advance of proliferating man and the ocean is smeared with emulsions in retaliation. Air is dangerous to all citizens for it has been abused to become a noxious gas to the prisoners of congestion.

Where have the leagues of untrapped meadows fled? Where is the sheep trail that linked Damascus to Jerusalem? Shrill iron machines sternly pound on steel tracking, propelled with the firing of coal and oil sucked and dredged from the graves of lost time. Astounding are the legions of man yet their faces are alike for man's countenance is plastic and shapes itself to the moment's void. Man is afraid to be alone with his soul.

Ponds and lakes that survived tens of peasant and indigenous city generations become, in less than a century, sour, dank, liquids putrefied by chemical infusions. Undulating hills that had sheltered the resting farmer and his plough team from the heat of noon are today riveted with miles of grave tablets. The city, daughter of spring and mother of autumn, is of winter today and shall be the mausoleum to the diseased Culture. The city has become a relic to itself, a temple in ruins. Streets steeped with the layered histories of kings and guild merchants, of lusty serf turned into sea quenched sailor, now parade placid clerks, overly emboldened matrons, any manner of defeated souls, and varied perverts.

Cleverness and eroticism do not begin to replace discarded family integrity. Where is the gain in giant and efficient machines when compared to the lost pride and purpose that has come to man? Futility is the product of our machine expertise and that it beguiles man with the odor of luxury is but a charade foiling hope.

Chapter 2

ARTISTS MUST NEVER dread to create beauty and drama. To create art a man must hate or love with a meticulous conflagration of awarenesses. Art exists to expand and fuel the inner being of man. Artists of any season but winter adorn reality with a vision of mankind as intense and emotional adventure. By the first decade of this century Western art had lost its confidence and direction. Impressionistic painting is the glaze on the patina of grandeur that is the Occident's soul disturbing beauty. It is of irony to observe the primordial art of hut peoples stand as the apogee of today's fashion. To seek the ardor of the West in the wood carvings of Jungian witch doctors is the punishment for venturing to encompass the earth with the wings of a mythical eagle. The Greek was not unwise to beware the success of the instant for on the dawning a man's pride may seek dishonour. As fell Daedalus, so dispirited and abashed became the peregrine that was the West. Aged bird drops precipitously in disorder to the flayed sea. The hunter bird turmoils the air in frantic exertion as she sees her conclusion below.

So fell the West. Without compassion, World History and Cultural morphology dull the desire to be detached of our bodies and instead be of the earth's rhythms. Yes, we are always chased back into the beginning seas. Those who do not assent to the loss of the West be uncomforted for there shall never be a poet born who can disguise this plummeting hurt. To change artifacts into the remarchings of dust kings is not of poetry but of a saddening.

To carpenter a ship is not a gesture of cowards. The Vikings were builders of tight craft. Their dragon ships brazenly attacked any and all. Without adventure man is inanimate and thus it was the Norse who melted energy into the crucible that was Europe. There must be a hunger to be greater than even a dream, if thee is to be but an irresolute plodder. The Cultures of man have been conceived by warrior races who, when confronted with sparsely populated plains, were sirened into rooting by the rivers hidden beneath the land. A luting is heard from the cultivated land and without fanfare the song chorals a birth of a people. Converted but recently to the land, they insist on further adventure, for their nomadic blood is but slowly coagulated.

After the winter of the River Culture various nomads advanced from the northern mountains and plateaus to claim suzerainty of the solidified forms of Egypt and Babylon. However these invaders had little interest in creative art or original thought. The most powerful of the warrior Empires of Asia, as clefted at the Hindu Kush, knew or cared not to construct the smallest temple. Zarathustra's simple and loving pleas for the Righteousness of the Ox Soul, to never be destroyed by the Lie, unfortunately offered the sybaritic Mede and Persian princes convenient aphorisms instead of the rigours of systematic religious practices. Slighter were the contributions of the several horsed empires to stylistic techniques for they were but rough imitators of the felled Egyptian-Babylonian World.

As man increased his stock and knowledge of the seasonal wraiths he feared less the darkness and traveled the earth in pilgrimages of discovery. It was the time in which the first Culture of men, River, had entered into the impotence of fraudulent armies and kings who collapsed at the spectre of aggression. A moment when mankind was amove uncharted to future shapings. We read of Isaac and Abraham but how many other patriarchs of earth's divers peoples have been unrecorded. The crescent of the East honeyed the warrior cavalries to her in rapid succession. Man's first fertile lushness as form had not the cataphracts of a later age to protect the fertile valleys. With a sudden devastation the horsed barbarian took the Culture's sapped structure as tribute. This plaster shell of power curtained the vacancy left by the Culture's death.

It was to the Hebrews with their outlawed Lord of One

who offer a fragrance remembered from this lethargic interlude. They were desert wanderers and neither child nor mother to the Culture of their time. The Jews did not state art, science, or logic but they did have faith in a blessing God never idol or fetish. Moses and Zarathustra organized not a Culture or empire but they reside as fragments of man's experience as learning and teaching, of love as hope.

The Greek embarks not out of Asia or from that tainted island of Egyptian civilization that lay off the peninsula, Crete. He came from the interior of Eurasia, out of the region near where came the flooding of mankind as portrayed by the Indo-European. Dorians chanted their strident battle cry into the chapters of history. From the mountain spurs of northeast Greece these savages conquered the Peloponnesus. They shut the eyes of the Mycenaen and Archaen actualities, no more would the legends of the Heroes be enacted by living men. Now a poet's skill must give motion to the children of the Gods. That the Ionic is thought to be the grace of that which Greece was, is an incomplete lyric. Both Athens and Sparta were spermed by the Doric sword. For the exploits of the warrior unleashed an expansive vitality in the hearts of the elder peoples of the land. The Dorian rejected the Minoan civilization though they did take technique from the island and shore formations. These clannish men of war adapted little from the fibrous Egyptian world. The River Culture's enhancement of the physically dead and its dread of the future was inimical to the audacious Greek who burned his fallen comrades but revered their spiritual remembrance. Ionic souls were captured entotal by the Dorian mystique. And thusly if a boy dreams it is of adventuresome kings and not of mummies capitaled by their pyramids. The Greek identification is to the Doric infantryman and without this allegiance to belligerence Hellas would not have known Athens.

Athena the Goddess is a woman-man, a guardian spirit and a general of a highrock of a city. The moon holds no terror for her majesty of courage. Athena is the son-daughter of the Doric soldier and the Ionic husbandman. Utilizing the techniques that the Egyptianized Cretans had exhibited in their mastery of matter, the Ionians, when injected with the blood of the Dorians, begat the Greek. On the beaches of Asia's crown this new man was free to remould his ethos, his pneuma, and directly was issuing novel ideas and visions across the Aegean to the peninsula and back again to the islands and shore colonies.

Why was it that the Dorics were bearers of a Culture while other savage peoples portaged salt? Perhaps this may be explained by time's juxtaposition but even if this question can never be deciphered, the realization was sublime. Egypt was an antique scar when on the promontory that was the stone and thin soil of Greece, a phoenix soared to announce that a newer Culture of man lived.

Undoubtedly it was the quicksilver combination of Doric and Ionic ego that furnaced the Culture but what served as causal? Who can fathom what draws one people to immortality and their neighbor to oblivion. Certainly there must be laws and rules, inverse and direct, that predict the birth of Cultures but I find only poetic symbols to depict beginning deeds. I know not where to mine the proofs but if a man be patient with his dreams he might uncover the road of the Greeks.

Mankind's tale executes no clearer conflict, no sharper definitions between competing epochal moments than that of the jealous Greek cities waging war against encroaching Asia. Historians from Herodotus through today have maljudged the strengths of the two contestants. To think that the victory of the Greek is unacountable or surprising is to see the conspicuous and not the essence. Licentious deceit and venality would have had to be present in heavy coined archers amongst the Grecian fleet for warriors of a Cultural summer to allow themselves to be defeated by a debilitated relic of the Egyptian era. Accept as fact when the father of history speaks of two million boat-bridging the Hellespont. Numerically superior hosts have battle advantage when they are comparable in desire to the inferior opponent. Xerxes might have come with half again his horde and defeat still would bitter his breath. The Greek was in supreme condition, bodily and spiritually, while the Persian was listless and historically played out.

That Asia came to Greece is the result of myopic blindness. The house royalty of Persepolis were, as sightless as the lords of Cathay, who in the West's summer misinterpreted those tiny companies of Europeans that poked here and there. Men of a Cultural summer gain success in their undertakings by their confidence. The ease of the Greek or Western ascendancy was not because of better weapons or of proficiency but that the vanquished could not match their spirit of bold aggression. Lands too youthful or ancient in spirit succumbed to the possessive vitality of the surging Cultures. Only when pitted against the older but viable Arabian autumn did the West meet rejection for any period of time.

The city states of Greece defeated the Persian Immortals and massed infantry with improbable dismissal. Actual battle was of less difficulty than the problem of unifying the egotistic cities into a common weld. Mischievous and envious, the Greek expected a devious tenor in all transactions. Victory over Asia is not astounding but that Athens and Sparta could fight as allies and serve under each other's generals approaches the incredulous. A paramount state was not to appear among the Greeks until the outlanders of Philip's Macedon seized authority. Alexandrian hegemony was predicted at Salamis yet how great a vastness is between the summer triumph and the winter colossus a bare century and half separated.

The Grecian warriors of the phalanx who fought at Marathon and later at Plataea had no super weapon but they did have an inner aggressiveness that was unmatched in warfare. Sword against sword is suspense but sword clashed with spirit is intoxication. The Will of the Greek ethos was immeasurably stronger than the extenuated power of several Persian worlds. It is the Greek fate that the rivaled walled cities could not comprehend a combined prowess except in the last recital that was linked by Alexander. The Greeks had but one overwhelming tactic in life, a sense of individual pride that genitaled great warriors and encompassing tragedians. Haughty Athens birthed much of the Hellenic legend in art and war. It is fact that her finest attainments were actualized in the periods when she was far from being a purified democracy. However, Athens persevered thru generations a sense of justice that created an atmosphere of freedom that saw her citizens speak and live in dignity. That a third of her populace was neither slave nor mendicant is of human society in growth by experience. Pericles resisted the temptation to grant the franchise promiscuously to all the inhabitants of Athens' short lived empire. And if in doing this thing of reaction he helped invalid his city's spore, he also was true to the Greek rationale that the city is of the most secret personal matters.

Odysseus was bred to self-reliance and independence when such terms were of feral potency and not masks of pretense. His Gods taught sexuality as a divinity and thus he is afraid of entangling depths as they have no limits in space. To be champion at Olympus fair is painfully worked for by Spartan king or island poet, leaving gluttony to the barbarians.

Epicurean modes are apology for weakening Cultural restraint, as Stoicism is the alertly chiseled features of the aristocrat as he contends the buffets of winter. As Socrates is the stone cutter teacher of summer, so Plato is the articulate master of autumn, and in finality Aristotle is the closing repository of the Greek contribution. Aristotle is the masterpiece of intellectual summation and extrapolation but there is no poetry in his inspection of man and his world.

In dealings of ordinary practicality the Greek was dishonest and a dissembler, except with his family, which in many instances, he also considered his home city as blood relative. Demanding self-advancement as a salutation to his pride, he lies and pillages without hesitation of conscience. His women were brooms to be attended to only in their role as mothers of sons. To clean the hearth and breed heirs was their station in the closeted circle of his needs. Adoring the sun and its secured but unencumbered liberty, he barely tolerates the night and its ever present totem, women. A representation of love to a woman was never discernible in any of the Greek seasons and was indeed quite infrequent. Helen's seizure bespeaks tomes of the despoliation that the man of the polis placed on the covenant between his woman and himself.

To lift a shield with unapparent confidence and smash it onto the skull of the enemy was the Greek's method of gaining the admiration of those whom he sought approval from, his comrades in the phalanx or on his oar. To tend the olive grove and wine arbor in feelingful cultivation was the healthy seasoned Greek's patrimony to the Gods. To keep Olympus content as his father's father had was of duty but goodness and truth were not. To run the swift race naked under the unshadowed sun. To win or to lose but always to extend the body to fullest exertion is the goal. With lungs battering the chest as he waited, still swaying from the course, to be circled with the olive wreath, this then was to be the Greek.

Chapter 3

A BARBARIAN'S WORK is not the creation of sailing ships. A people in growth must take each step singularly, and some backward in punishment for arrogance and disdain. A call from the sea came to the men of Attica and the response to let flow the seed of their city into the boards and oars of a deckless craft was not an act of cowardliness. Setting a lonely linen sail on a lean mast as the waves arrow, headed with tipped spray, sounded throughout the wooden planks was not the action of fearing maidens.

Few have been the peoples of earth who have sailed the outer parts of the caprioling sea. The larger share of man find the seas as presences without protracted meaning or effect. Yet the sea is an authoring spirit and to those who esteem inquiry above callow acceptances find enrichments of challenge in the thunderous motion. Through the ages it has been repetitive that the waters of salt are malicious and cruel, but it is false to think this, for the oceans are the messengers of sentient life. The seas are Gods that lifted recognition from the caves of the primordial become. Life is of the beginning always, without the mighty sea this world of experience and fact would not have been brought forth. All prelife is death, nothing sprouts life but yesterday. Life announces that death has voiced its noteless dirge. The sea, pounding, set in fructifying movement by the soundless star, collided with the rock and in a consuming despair created an intactness of life. Man's adventure began with the groan of the splitting stone.

Watch the Greek ship captain, face guarded by beard and bronze helmet, an opaque profile against the dusk as he arches his hand to the first glint of star. With an unthought gesture he tosses an unripened grape as sacrifice to sun and sea. The Greekling sailor may well be the quintessence of mystery's meaning for man.

History can be sensed by the acknowledgment of the apriori existence of this present moment's experience. To accept that which has become the past as adjacent to each instant of reality gifts extraordinary vision to the beholder. In this bitterest of seasons mankind lunges away from the become in rejection of the past and its implication of decay. Winter man has exercised his historical retrospection in order to misnote all that once was the becoming, to arrange a pacific reply to this age.

Columbus's sailing of his craft in search of India is momentous adventure. His verve results in the annexation of two continents to the West en masse. Acres of untouched farming land, slumbering until the Spaniards initiate a window to Europe. Without the Spanish and Portuguese to subjugate the Americas, today's New Europe was but a coast for vagrant sea folk to visit and forget.

To set sail, to lift heavily grained oar to push outward into Salamis bay is a dictum of history as compelling as a child's Will that demands the body to hold itself upright, erect. The design was bold, either one flees or stays to fight Asia in the shore crowded waters. Persia is almost spared by the jealously competitive Greek but Themistocles is perfection and consorts the fates. He shouts a coveted whisper to the Persian fleet standing at the straits, and the Asians habited to Greek mendacity, respond to seal the remaining exits from allied retreat. Now the men of Athens, Sparta, and all the rest, less arrant Thebes, must cease polemics and wage a great battle. Son of mighty Darius, blood of immortal and founder Cyrus, peacock Xerxes is enthroned to view the conflict but is hurried away as the groans signal the rupture of his pretense invasion. Salamis abrades the Greek Culture onto the glass blocks of World History. A sizable golden bowl is offered Delphi in thanks for the oracle's declaration to trust in walls of wood. Yet the priests erred for it was the Greek's boldness and determination that safeguarded the spirit of Hellas. Those of Salamis were entirely the sons of Achilles for though wounded and maddened by the deadly pierce of the ruinous blades of Troy, they refuse to admit their fate.

Have you befriended a man free of the fear of the Gods and are you cognizant that the Gods were enamoured of a people? If thee answers yes, then you have known the Athenian of yore. Foolish are those who try and rob Western man of his acquired heritage of Homer. Both Greece and the West are bloodied in the spurting sperm of violent embrace. European man has held to the mystique of the idealized Greek and in the eros of living has projected him as his mother. Western man is conscious of the tenuousness of the relationship and is emotionally pledged to the constant proving of its authenticity. He suffers with this identification to the Greek and alternately feels guilt and joy because of it. There can be no elaboration of spirit between the two Cultures for they are immersed in differing justifications. Always there are similar responses to uniform stimuli but it is in the act and thought of solution that the separation between Cultures is noticeable.

An intermingling of Cultural characteristics in some few aspects does take place. The term transference seems to define this state of connection. Essentials of fact from opposing Cultures do transfer across time as a continuum. These tools and techniques are grafted to the root of the coming newness. That which enters the river of the West from the sea of Athens besides fact is a concept of self that is imitative of the independent aristocrat. In both Greece and in Europe there existed a ceaseless demand for expansion. In the Hellas this was pronounced in the colonization of daughter cities, while in the West there was evidenced a desperate, seemingly biological, need for fulfilment of geographic and dynastic potentialities. From the constricted states of Athens, Corinth, and Sparta a niagara of economically excessed citizenry sailed to lands where they gladly settled into established, mother polis, conformities.

Rome's empire is the inheritance from Alexander pruned by time into an exquisite obesity. The Greek began his fabled growth as a creator of Cultures when he formed his son to mother-bride attachment with his city. To some extent this type of fidelity is indicated in the precocious cities of the West as districted in northern Italy. This love for city is the donation the Greek bestows on inanimate structure in lieu of what he does not accord to his women. Roman imperialism is symptomatic of the wasting away of the earlier bonds to the city as a world complete. It is the Greek's eros for the city that impels the Athenian founting in stone and word. This impassioned affection he implanted into the mortar of his city was the inspiration for the Culture of Greece.

City became the cause and result of the Classical World. This innate regard for city is not absent from the beginnings of the West. The inchoate European city was soon festooned with the sculptor's and architect's plan. Citizens of any Culture exhibit a reverence and communion with the city as an integral repository for their pridefulness. However, the cities of Greece and Europe have neurons of vastly different purposes. The Greek asks no more of the Gods than that he and his polis may prosper and never be enslaved. While the Western as a disciple of a heavenly King and His Prince, Christ, has an innocent trust in the presence of monarchy and kingdom. A city to the Greek is both temple and lover, and if the Gods belong to all men indiscriminately the city is a gift granted specifically by birth. The Spartan warrior leads the world's most estimable armies against all opponents yet theirs was a scantily walled and templed town. Still this rather vegetated polis could call the Greek souled Lacedaemonian home from the voluptuous and luxurious Asiatic courts. Athenian bred Xenophon was captivated by the Spartan manner of life and he chose their code as his own from a candid admiration. The potency of the Spartan "way" is discernible into the Punic Wars, as General Xanthippus proved in the defeat of Regulus by Carthaginian forces under his command.

Incredible Alcibiades, as if he were an unamused God, watches from his sea cliff perch as the fleets of Sparta and Athens ram. His Athenian brothers listened not to his incisive advice for they thought him to be liar to his home after a life of traffic with the Asians and Lacedaemonians. Foolish

Athens to forget that he was loved by both his instructor Socrates and his truer father than if blood, great Pericles. Alcibiades in being fearless of Hermes' wrath, by striking the stone member off, was forever of Athens' bravado and but reflected her tempestuous personality and golden luster by his arrogant actions. Swollen skulled Pericles was the best Athenian in most things and not the least so when he outrages the Demos by loving his whore publicly and daring to open his house to her. Envious was the Greek and incapable of respecting greatness unless it be one's own.

To be hero to their city was quite sufficient grandeur to these upstart Greeks. They judged an empire or kingdom barbaric institutions scaled to a city in freedom. For the West the city was a stage of growth, a level to reach and surpass. Kingdoms became the European vessel of political, historical, and Cultural completion. But to those of the Greek seas, from Propontis to Syracuse, the marbled city was man's most regal offering.

Chapter 4

SAVAGES FROM THE rivers Elbe, Seine, and Rhine torched the remains of the Roman world. The Churches of Constantinople and Antioch survived the onslaught but Peter's Rock was torn from earth and when it shuddered to stillness it was not of Athens or Jerusalem or of Caesar's Rome but was now of an angry barbaric Tiber and Guadalquivir. From New Rome an adherence to Christ's birth was impressed into the emerging European Culture.

Germanic peoples swelled throughout the places of imperial Rome and slaughtered the shades of Hellas. Their crude iron axe was of peculiar weight when struck upon the Roman's armor. There could not be a relationship but of warfare between the Roman world and the German peoples.

Jesus was issued as a spring flower from the corpulent decomposition of the Classical world. From the age of Empire Christ arose as indeed the Saviour of man for the Latin civilization had come to the Mediterranean in a most terrifying costume. After Carthage is extinguished from actuality Roman power has no competitor and flows in brutal haste to stockade the lands encompassing the middle sea. Rome is without grace or redemption yet man seeks both qualities in order to endure as man. At insignificant Judea an exultant commitment to a mysterious God of deliverance remained, though the people had been corrupted by Hellenic and Roman subjugation. Obstinate, the Jew surrendered not his Lord to the Greco-Roman sophists. A teacher is revealed and He offered atonement to all men, especially the downtrodden, administered with a blessing of love. Christianity as a faith opposed to that of a religion is anchored on the bed rock of Judaic salvation. All the accoutrements and modes that formed the Pagan's method of worship are but chaff to be threshed away on that desert boulder.

Christ is of the east, He is enticed by the West and made her Son. His spirit was first apparent in the lands of the River Culture ages before Athens was a villaged fortress. For although Jesus could have been birthed only at the juncture between Cultures, He is not of morphological rhythm and His relevance is to those of any season's world an imprint of yet another thread in the history of man.

Christ's twelve and their students found the corpse that was the Grecian world destroyed as an abomination. The Christian Church of the Roman winter is a victory of Will over fate and historical propensity. That a monotheistic devotional faith could burgeon during the last decay of antiquity is astounding in its lesson for this ineffectual moment. It is difficult to map the chaotic conditions of late Rome but it is clear that the Church's endurance is not a happening of the period's vacuum but a resolute act of human discipline and Will sustained in the calamitous disintegration of a social entity. Centuries pass before the Christ is received by the wind worshipping Germans. The Church itself changes drastically as she asserts herself in the realm of actuality in leading the barbarians into acceptance of possibly kinder paths.

The peoples, the cities, and the art of Athens are unregenerative in this world of Western manufacture. Homer and Euripides exist only as do the fragments of shattered clay pottery, pieces of baked earth that are of a lost abstraction of justice. Poets as Sappho are no more than a few loosened pages escaped from Alexandria's charcoaled rolls. Lines that in spite, or because, of their brevity become dreams that guide man to enter freely into the imaginations of Greek art and thought.

Spartan warriors are maligned by impressions false and contrived by Western manipulators to the misrepresentation of their heroism as paranoiac. If thee could join me on the flight of my vision at Thermopylae, that place where the Lacedaemonians were slain, then thou might also see the shield walled phalanx as a dance aglow with the spirit of a mighty age. Here at this quiet pass curled by the sea the Greek gained by his own idealization as fact. Antiquity was confirmed as a Homeric saga in this skirmish. Sparta was late at Marathon but her cup was filled at Thermopylae and at Plataea. Those who admire the purity of Athens detest Sparta for the blemishes on her soiled swords. Yet in the crushing plunge of these blades there was an essence of truth as beauty, of the hunter's soul accomplishing the Culture's actuality.

Pericles stole from Delos the confederation's treasure and with it he celebrated Athens with a radiant shift of white marble and illustrious metals. Tragedy is the bread of life for without it men are but fools and fountains of lust. Pericles and the Spartans play a high drama backgrounded by their Culture's orgiastic burst of art. Intrinsic souls are dichotomies when Sparta confronts Athens in Cultural competitions. The two cities chase each other yet higher on Zeus's mountain in search of truth and courage's glory. And one city without the other is a lesser vase. It is the conflict of the emulating cities that inspires the Greeks to surpass their individual selves. Doric motifed temples and halls stand on the acropolis of Ionic Athens to culminate the Greek adventure for all of her champions. Sun bright was the columned Parthenon of Athens with interiors gold mirrored with the reflection of bright Attica.

Alas she is not of summer anon when a bolder man, fully configurated, defied the Gods' pride on stoa or at Olympic festival. Sad it is that the wood tiers lay as diffused atoms where once jousting crowds became somber as the chorus anviled the words of Aeschylus to the open sky. To have a place in the phalanx of the splendid doomed at Syracuse is to seek out an honoured death. The Greeks led their lives as fine adventure and returned to their odes truthful genius.

Book III

EAGER EUROPE

Chapter 1

EUROPEAN MAN in the summer of his creation began his search for a father. And in finding a savage as parent he fled from this fact of primitive origin in Christian shame and instead sought the paler mist of lost Athens to fashion a fallacious ancestor.

The infant West was plucked from the agony of a desolate land. Four hundred winters of anarchy and rapine preceded Charlemagne as the nomadic stocks plundered the felled civilization.

When the monks and accessory scholastics of the West misnamed their Culture's summer a renaissance, they dignified the fatuous quest to find a domesticated paternity to replace the marauding barbarians. That which was largely transferred from Athens to the Occident was of technique, of fact. The usage of Roman bureaucratic nomenclature by unlettered creatures has no historical meaning except to show that the Goths and Vandals were indeed savages. This use of Latin as base to their but forming linguas accords evidence to their social immaturity. Contracts and restrictions are known as law and as such belong to the sphere of fact and are interchangeable in differing eras. Laws are technical devices that control ever present human misbehavior. Murder or pederasty are identical crimes of social and personal defeat whether they take place in the Dynasty of Menes or in Brasilia. A law is man's barrier that he constructs to protect himself from himself. Laws are extant, palpable, tools that can be passed to many peoples and ages with facility. Application of law changes as to the condition, the season, of the society. And as demoralizing decay is effected, so the assiduity of structure weakens. Laws are progressive only as all fact is, by accumulation and refinement, not in creation or spirit. While a poem's partial stanza may be but a solitary sentence, it well can speak of the Lord's direction as any senate's legislation.

At the western channel of the mother sea waited the blackness of the Atlantic. To the north were fertile spaces from whence came wandering peoples as unsettled as the ocean's turbulence. Their world was of kingly oaks and of murky rivers and swamps. Their land was harsh and cold in comparison with the mildness of the parts surrounding the Roman sea. The Empire was ill and aged without resources but contemplation. The vengeful fates clamoured for retribution to punish the assuming Romans. And her Gods were fatigued, they unshackled the never late storm of expected death.

Christian priests of impoverished and diminished Rome listened not to the poetry of the routed Heroes and Gods for the old ways were proscribed. Albeit, the works of the philosophers were not censured as there was a need of trained logic to curb the abounding heresies. At Constantinople the documents of the Athenian age were preserved, the poetry and goat's song of that which was to be the Greek. Plundering but devout crusaders awoke the slumbering myths of Greek warriorhood, which invoked a sense of brotherhood in the evolving West. There were similarities of beginnings, of trials, and war's flame which did produce a concept of kinship. Starkly the Athenian pneuma stood out from the fact of Europe's savage nature. Christian guilt needed the Homeric legends of a greater man for they were welcome in a world that had no mything but the realism of giants Thor and Beowulf. In substance a luminosity of awarenesses separated the age of Delphi from that of Cluny.

There is not a progression in the actions of men but there does exist a humanity of poets, artists, sculptors, and tragedians who sing a harmony of sentient discoveries common to the inner worlds of any man. Those who are inspired to create art are excited by identical questions and introspections of actuality in any age. It is the quality of artists that marks the disparity of the seasons and not the passion of the creator's effort. For the nature of man challenged by the phases of aware living is the levin of poets. Supremacy of tragedy is omniscient in the alphabet of any honorable poet. Life may be joyous but the poet never escapes the reality that tomorrow may doom the princeling of this now.

Mankind has never learned from the past those examples that might affect change in the present. Yet if a being be courageous and thusly able to combat inevitable defeat, he could discern why his moment is warped as it is and then attempt to pioneer the paths ahead. History of men is a river in time, calibrated, but without sanctions except those of life and death. Material wealth can be expanded with the tools and techniques of Cultural accumulation. However that which magnifies the essential spirit of man into the observable phenomenon known as art has not progressed a micro dot in the ability to express love, hope, self-recognition, and defeat since the become was evidenced. Christ is not of art but of the soul's love, but art did ready man for his coming. Christ is a dictum of humanity in assent of love and gifting. When Europe took Him as their God, this alone changed mankind. His ethos, by the European consent, became of the peoples of the West.

The river that is man and the river that is history of the seasons create from their nexus an adventure that seers call the march. To be of this march is of energy and there does not have to be an ending or a result in justification for its length or difficulty. To step the road of destiny is of hardship and especially so during a time of Cultural disruption. A creative person, he may be prophet or king, leads the march. But every man of any station is born with the interior freedom to make this journey. Predictably, most men never venture the arduous labour that movement and change exact, for one must strenuously protest inertia and disconcern in order to make the pathing veer a slight degree.

To consent to one's self in inward frankness admits the concept of person. Simplicity is the opened lock to this state of personal acceptance. There is an uniquely lonely way to be traveled before the animal that is man dares to envisage his need as a soul that also is of man. The preparation needed to become a person is a search for love and awareness beyond the dread imbecility of the season. Say unto the fearful child that he must march on for to be totally human is to be a sea of living time, of a spirit not trapped by fear. Man is incompetent of Cultural fertilization except in seasons of prosperity. All men are found cowardly and ignoble when demands of independence and self-reliance are called for as man is self-blinded. Alone in his tense mentality but a few come forward out of their vital dimness with the soul exposed. When one dares to reveal a personal sanctity, the soul becomes as a candle that trumpets his brothers to the march.

To become a seer the soul shall be lanced by the examinations of reality and of the agony of personal exploration. Profound vision directs the proud man to continue the marching. They can not fail if tomorrow is to be won and gallant song is to be heard. Every man has a soul, even the self-blinded is inwardly garbed. Man is a moment of matter and as such eternal in a delicately wrought manner. He is animal that suffers pain that penetrates the outer cocoon's senses. From the ravages of soul astonishing visions of change are emitted. Sightings indicated with time flourishing and dying, with the winds that rise from the ocean currents to fondle the wetted earth.

Goethe and Bacon belong to the school boy's lessons and this empty season has dismembered eager Europe. This moment is hostile to the remembrance of the awakened spring, of the sun ripened orchards of summer, of symphonies of the autumnal silos. Music has been interred in the winter ground, entombed is the West forever vanished without a lingering kiss. Consumed in the wasted energies of a technology malformed and insane. The Culture's elegant being is rotted by an undisciplined industrial fungus. Western spirit may be sought in the swirling, chilled, nebulae of the become. Not quite leaf sheeted is her structure for she doth resist death though dead.

There are men of resolve who pronounce the West still animate and fecund. Disagreeable as it may be, these brave fellows must be refuted for Cultural disintegration is an unalterable counterpoint of life as actuality. These few insist that silence is a better protection than truth and indeed they are correct. This essay is not a perfumed emollient but hopefully is the horned oliphant that alarms. That this tale may promote futility and hasten inertness can not be disregarded. Yet may it not cause in its confession of decay a bulkheading to withstand this moment's despairing impetus. Never is this prose voiced to hurry my Culture's becoming. And these words are not styled adroitly for fame's burst. Grieving at the West's downfall, I fear the fashion of her final throes. Even a powerless person must ask the mallets to halt and that purposeless factories inhibit their pointless productions. For if their materialistic offspring but serve to increase the soul's discomfort, then they must be redirected into meaningful programs.

Conflict is the essence of artistic creation, as failure is its goad and as defeat is intrinsic to discovery. Passion and agony are not commercialized word sounds to be abused by mercenary word technicians. Rather they are symbols that represent the ingredients due man's love of hope. It is apparent that this book gives not strength to the aged pillars of the West and in my vehemence to admit light into this prison maze I do set them to shaking. And though I do desire to rush the approaching spring, I never wish to destroy or maim any cloth remaining to the Western Culture. Desperate appears the future but this day still holds strands of a tapestry that should be hoisted as a banner that leads man as he marches onward.

Neither soul despising communism nor socially unconcerned capitalism can satisfy the inner needs of man. Winter socialism condemns the world to the political, economic, and artistic censorings of a confused mass's judgments and values. Cultural springs are formed by the men of the plow. It is the aristocrats as vigorous kings who lead the developing Culture to success or failure. By the days of decline the nobility is decrepit and victim to lassitude. Numerous peasants have been forced off or have fled the toil of the land to metamorphically change into the deprived mob that longs for vengeance. Patently abused by the unaware criminality of the industrial, social retrogression, men are quick to shed previous adherence to God and king for opportunity of material well-being and security. Indeed the Roman Empire expired with the barbarian-slave controlling the city and the emperor's chair. Admittedly the infusion of the combative, acculturated, barbarian allowed the empire to persist for several additional centuries of strife.

Only trivial arrogance and degradation remain to the royalty of Europe as all trappings of power have been forfeited. The proletarian assumption of command is the result of Cultural attenuation and is not in any way a consequence of environmental accident or historical progression. Marx's synthesis of world history as economically determined is the stuff of tragedy and not of logic as pertained to the continuous concept of World History. As Brooks Adams' theory of material and artistic energy enfeebling into economic cheapness, Marx arrives at a perspicacious view of his season's degradation. The search for correctives as applied to the contemptible squalor of the industrial worker's conditions drove this outraged soul to invalid historical conclusions. But Marx did provision efficacious methods that instigated the "lower depths" into remedial activity.

Proletariat administration of power does tend to prolong the existence of moribund societies but only by the infusions of brutal over simplifications. Communism is disclosed as ritual that ignored the individual, but fought the cruelties of proliferating industrialism, but under structures that would compensate the masses with dignity and influence. Others of contemplation such as Saint-Simon, Fourier, and Rousseau investigated both utopias and escapisms fabricated on rejection of technological excess. In a spirit of faith they searched for acceptable substitutes to counter the collapsing West. Terrible injustice and avarice had pervaded the Culture's treatment of her peoples. An infamous neglect of the serfdom community was now considered the normal social condition. If communism is the shroud of the dead Culture, then uninterested and unaware self-interest is the weaver of the garment.

Communism and capitalism, while appearing to be opposing precepts, are but symptoms of the same malady, Cultural decline. Each dictum has fanatical adherents who desire to plunge continents into maniacal warfare. Neither understands that they are related responses to a fractured order. By use of propagandized terms and generalizations of heavy emotional content they divide again the already dismembered society. Socialism is the West's false rhapsody, a pretense of progression toward a reverie that camouflages static art, an omnipotent governmental apparatus, and a rejection of love and soul.

Chapter 2

RELEASE AND FREEDOM are separate and competitive concepts of man's state of being. Historically, release attends the failure of a sustained immortality as to the social constructions of man. Tradition and discipline are replaced by universal balloting, which in the winter morass serves only to depreciate the total establishment. Discipline, the superstructure of a creative people, is derided in the age of release. A connection between that political governing placebo known as unbridled democracy and that circumstance of man in fatigue that may be termed release is apparent for both are cankers of a Culture in sickness. Dictators and emperors are the aftermath of societies relinquished of character and loyalty. Tyrants are the infants of the Demons. It is not a question respecting man's multiformity and legal equality, collectively or individually. But it is necessary, however remorseful, to be aware that democracy in its final stages is a prerequisite of empire and totalitarianism and is a result of Cultural morphology. The hope of democracy is sublime but the sentiment itself is a reaction to failed form and spirit. Power is assumed by the most numerous class only when the inner workings of traditional government have collapsed into regulations benefiting only the propertied and moneyed class. This debacle leaves all men burdened with malevolence. Incredibly, it well may be in the last comparisons of defeat that the aborting dictatorship or empire improves the condition of the numerous labouring class as paralleled to the choice of anarchy's scourge.

Freedom is Apollo lashing his fiery animals to close day in a concerto of sparks. Release is the shootings of the Romanovs and the banishment of Themistocles. Restraint is the powered discipline of the idea of a Holy Roman Empire to involve men in great schemes and efforts. Freedom is Galileo seeking the sun's secrets and Copernicus charting the stars in spite of the Church's displeasure. One may be king or artisan, a man shall perform his destiny in keeping with Cultural development. Innovative and as original as the master composers were they created within the traditions of Western art. Their tonal arrangements electrify the listener with songs that began with the balladeers of manor hall.

In the kinetics of the West's soul a repeated demand for freedom is maintained. It is not to be free only of despots, unjust conditions and want, but a fervency to be liberated from the corporeal and from death. A wondrous view of space and time existed in the blush of the Culture and to this twilight of now for even the slattern's soul demands to lift free from reality and be of God. Freedom is of two compartments, of leaving a negative circumstance and a reaching out to an exalted hope.

The story of European man is piped by a soldier boy in martial strophe. Angry and threatening are the sounds of the West's footsteps, for his sword is never confined to scabbard. Release as typified in modern war is condoned slaying for the weapons are ruthlessly superior to any warrior's elan. Mad priests slaughter well but the dictators nested from the revengeful multitude are the masters of devastation. The revolutionary armies of France are reaction to the deterioration incarnate to the maxims of Cultural morphology. The reigns of the later Bourbons were indeed abysmal and in fact they quite deserved to be deposed. Some abatement of injustice did result from the deeds of the militant citizenry of France and there was a relevant glory in the voice of the mob emancipated and uplifted as expressed in their paean, the Marseillaise. Unfortunately, their cannons foretold more than a monarchy's death.

To blend England and Normandy into one kingdom was William the Bastard's ambition. This springtime prince and the winter tyrants are removed by not only the years but by apriori perceptions of life and its significance. Pious and pensive William was unlettered and of a tanner's blood but his was a kingly soul. Brilliant in restraint, he controls his rage while his locust of a first son plots and acts to supercede his ducal father. Great is William who charges his men to foe gusty Harold.

William and Hitler are placed on opposing points of the West's spectrum. And as extremes they seem to embrace similar appearing objectives. Each is persuaded to the alloyage of antagonistic lands into monolithic solidarity and both essay audacious invasions and campaigns. However, the dictator coils and strikes in spasms of insane loathing for man. Normandy's credulous Duke patrons houses for the servants of Christ and brings stimulation to Western Europe. William forbade not the Jews to come to England, where indeed they found little haven. But the Bastard prohibited them not and he may have encouraged the Rouen Jews to send their colony.

Ineffable demons stalked the forests and flats of Europe until they surfaced grotesquely in winter's harshness. The Jew is ever catered to the fiends as a burnt offering sacrifice. Because of their placement in Europe's history, the Iron Ovens of the dreaded concentration camps can not be approximated to any other satanic deed of the faltering Culture. At no point and in no hour did European man fail himself as he did in this crude futility. As if the absurd doctrine that permanence may be brought to earth by the systematic killings of passive children and their traumatized parents. Taken in context, numerically and historically the decimation of the European Jew is not an inordinate crime for there are lengthier lists of man's savagery to those he terms stranger. But as an obscene tableau, the pits of emaciated cadavers tympani the wretchedness of a Culture in the extreme frustration of sensing its own death and unable to ignore its fear. No, it is not the enormity or even the fashion of their removal that must grieve, rather it is the how of it that stuns. To enslave nations of Blacks is counted a crime a century before the incident of the Ovens. Sadistic conduct toward the lower animals is censured decades prior to the Ovens. A humanitarian version of society termed Fabian socialism is embarked on years in advance of the Ovens.

Unhoped for progress in the prevention of disease begins long before the incredible furnaces. Thus it is the chronological moment that shocks and horrifies men of good will. The actuality of the Ovens predicates Cultural leprosy. The soul of the Culture is outraged by the immolations for every man is reduced with the cremated Jew.

The level of disappointment that a winter Culture must expect is in inverse proportion to the degree of success reached in its halcyon days. In the morns of fair breezes and yet deeper into the centuries when the leaves become sallow and black tinted, European man was capable of rebounding from any calamity. He has lost that regenerative Will and his physical aspect is palsied and he no longer can hold the perishing Culture upright.

Religious utopias are slain with their clockmakers and government is a weapon to be menaced by the alienated classes in this stifled era. Insular Britain of the nineteenth century midwifes the West's last calming pause before the cataclysm. Though Parliament existed and was supple, it was a house of fraudulent pennants, for the English aristocracy ruled and moulded the world's posture using Parliament only as a convenient auxiliary. Because the English nobility persisted, Britain was able to provide energy to the Culture concomitant as the continental became debased and atrophied.

Kings become magnificent only when they ignite a sense of expansion in their vassals. Louis the Sun king was effective not because of an overabundance of wisdom but because he was able to alert a belief in historical grandeur into his nobility. Xerxes is murdered by his bedchamber slaves not for the failure in Greece or his seduction of his brother's wife and daughter but because he had not a great dream to share with his aristocrats. A man of majesty may well be a libertine but he also must have faith in himself and his star. This is the kingly necessity and if he holds to it he shall be increased by the authority of his viscounts. Philip of Spain, he of the ascetic, martyred, portrait as a Western king of summer, invokes in his men an international involvement with history's thrust.

The word, "release" is used to express circumstances particular to the Cultural seasons of autumn and winter. It tells of disjointed souls and forsaken odes. Traditional modes and cohibitions of social restraint are abused by permissive relaxations. Today's art reproduces the moment's turmoil and rejection of man's inward reality. The European late autumn, the last few decades of the previous century, welled with a grand surge of impressive art. The West was dying but in a dynamic conquest of Will over organic failure she stood momentarily as luminous and energetic.

Winter's art is an outpouring of meaningful hate and of sensitive human shrinking from a corruption of values and idealization that seem worthless elements in a world gone mad. Contemporary man withdraws from this existence of sophist technology and ethics. His inner world is a reflected disorder of his actuality. Cultural release as decay is the reason for an acceptance of heretofore forbidden gratifications and self-induced euphorias. Cultural morphology is the pronouncement of atrophy and man retches in the humiliation of his bewilderment.

At Paris, in the years 1793-94, but twenty-five hundred heads were scissored from awareness yet this paltry butchery closed summer's eve as much as Rome's eradication of Corinth or Caesar's genocidic practices against the tribes of Gaul and Germany. The destructions of scores of thousands of Catholics, Protestants, Swedes, or Poles are plausible and explainable in historical perspective of the European dynastic and reformational wars, but to kill the French nobility by the use of a "modern" device glares out as Cultural motion in release. Summer's deflation was unnoticed for the entering autumn was resplendent.

European man seized the entire planet and made prisoner many impressive peoples. Among his captures were the plains and plateau natives of the Americas who are enticed into besotten degradation as the West masticates their wealthy lands. The Europeans' entrance into relatively naive societies rents the future of one elementary spring. To contemplate the might-have-been of the Inca-Aztec world if their tomorrow had been left is more than conjecture. The men of the West zestfully break the portals and as they feed their desires the appetite is not assuaged. As the triumphant Moors are thrown into retreat by the West, Asia is soon ravished by the European. In disquiet the West swims the veins of these dissimilar civilizations with results of wretched upheaval.

The poet's song is extreme and unsure in the now of this become. A vessel brave is held by threads of nugatory to the lapsed station of decayed time. Never shall the cockleboat wrestle the ruffled shoals anticipatory below the restless swells. Exile is the promise of the creator, self chosen or socially inflicted, for in the age of release disciplined awareness is mocked.

Slowly did the summer promenade toward the blotching shade, and at last it became as if lulled after a wayfaring imperiled. The dawning lights that were prodigious in creative potency are shuttled. The scholars were timid before the organic summer, they disapproved their own exhilaration and lettered the surging as a renaissance. Abject self-deceivers were they for there had not been a rebirthing of the Athenian way in Milan and Florence. European man had procreated a birth of historic dimensions. A giant tree she was, an amplification of accelerated growth. The expanding awareness never exceeded the limits of restraint during the elevating seasons. The Culture functioned with incredible energy and soon a world was made vassal.

Civilization is the embalmment of Cultural spirit. What appears as huge and conclusive is rather the withered skin of artifact that had contained a blessed seed. This now is an age of a too rapid communication of fact subtracted of spirit and truthfulness. Mechanization overran the West's judgments and values before the Culture understood that a catastrophe had taken place. Dostoyevski set forth the disaster, as he could not accept a future postulated on the abusement of a solitary child. Yet it was allowed even in the most prolix of the "progressive" Western nations, Great Britain. English children crawled on scabrous limbs down unlit, fume reeking, coal tunnels, exerting their frailness to dry up sacks of fossilized carbon to the surface's cruelties.

The churches did not disclaim this despoliation of their children, the kings said nothing and all in all none spoke except the poets. But they railed at the ominous stolidity with deserved rage. The poets failed not their integrity as they fought a technology that was without purpose except as to dreams that are of material bombast.

Serf and peasant flocked to the fetid quarters of the defiled cities where selfpride was discarded as too onerous a ballast. Man increased many fold in the city warrens. Immunities to the plagues had been acquired and science had begun to invade the lairs of the blights but grievous faults began to appear in the foundation stones of the Culture.

European science enabled man to control the reality that is of nature. Artisans of springtime had been adept at using mechanical aids as wind and water powered tools and with these inventions Europe started to regulate and divide labor into specializations. By the twelfth and thirteenth centuries windmills, rudders, and window glass were in use. However as the Culture outgrew the bloom of spirit, a summoning to technology substituted the potentialities as evidenced in art and form. Man placed himself in a debilitating contest with the machine and soon was struggling for survival in that most alarming competition. Once highly individualistic, European man has ensnared himself in the vagaries of a tool and power dominated setting. Men of this sunless age have enamoured themselves with a lust for technology above all else in their hyper-need for inanimate objects. And they care not of the portenting tomorrow that this perversion of wisdom shall bring.

Chapter 3

FREEDOM IS A REQUIREMENT of spirit that is brother to content awareness of being. It is an abstraction ranking in clarity to the essence that is the sky. Freedom is a weave of sheerness, a brocade of love laced with destiny. Freedom can not be found where the soul is sparse. Man alone experiences a state of perpetual liberation that is far grander than any law of nature. Some moment in the lost days before there was a temple anywhere, God and man Willed together that men shall be separate from the mists of the glen and cloud freckled plain. And it was then that man recognized the sleepless urging that was his inner self begging to be liberated from sea and earth. Essentials of awareness can not be brought to actuality unless conflict is dared. Fear is the antagonist of freedom. Inward liberty is not a balanced consent between soul and animal. Freedom is joined to Will as is wine to glazed pottery, for if divorced, each is empty of meaning. Few words suggest the achievements of man as does this exalted term, freedom. It paints a threshing apart from fear and a flutter of wing that ignores the absence of the stars. An essence alive, it evades the disease of Cultural decline and plays amongst the men of winter's gloom. Softened, weakly, souls deep in obeisance may eventually show resistance if the light of freedom searches and finds refuge in their hearts.

Emmanuel Ringelblum was besieged by the buffets of winter's fury yet his soul sang with freedom's gallantry. He, a Hebrew, chose to stay in the death stenched ghetto of Warsaw in the Time of the Ovens. He stayed not to punish his happenstance of birth with a false martyr's wile or to find a renunciation of the Lord and life at a brute's hands. Emmanuel remained in order to act out his inner convictions as a being of free Will, as dedicated to the becoming liberation of mankind though his brothers are enslaved. Ringelblum recorded the fatigue and ennui of spirit trapped by fate's damnation. And in that immense defeat of Will's hope he chronicled those few who were exorcised to a mighty defiance. The becoming spring, still distant, shall note that Western man's soul blazed with freedom though helpless in agonies and extremities. That the despised Jew could commend hope and faith in life's generosity while in bondage to the iron furnaces carols a dominion of freedom.

Liberation filled Emmanuel's soul when he accepted his decision irrevocable. Freedom is a choice of being and this chronicler stayed because his inner dazzlement was thankful to God and his own children for life's actuality. To be constant to one's self is the assent of freedom. To explore for that which is nobility and when locating it not to be ashamed. Concording a vow to remain proud and to honour though inequality and misfortune are thy bread in freedom's cult. To stand apart and cry thy love of light when the darkness is to be of elation. To stand, not to run and hide when you are cast into the charnel house of despair and madness is to be truly free. To walk the forgotten spring and hear the faint tunes is to be blest with the confirmation of freedom. Liberty is when all else has been extinguished except a single flash that defeats the impossible. To Will a newer spring into World History omens liberation as a poem of time as motion.

Liberty is an orange papered, wood crucified, kite soaring on a light string line. The boy runs the swooping toy to the lower breeze. His eyes liquid with the day's shine, he races the paper bird into the expectant sky. Gyrating and darting to be separate from its perpetual cord, the kite takes the boy's hand to the infinite, to the soul's freedom.

Cultures express their freedom in summer spires if they be Gothic ramparts or the Towers of Babylon. In the season of breasting vigor men of faculty bear creations that symbolize freedom. These men recite a hymn of tenacity. Newton, Tycho Brahe, and Palestrina grow copiously in the humus of summer. They cape the bulling darkness with filaments of insight. These singers of fruition cadence the parade to full gait and prompt man to movement and introspection. In the West's beginnings the rhyme makers lifted a refrain to the clouds. European man heard and energized his inert hulk to employment. Primordial mud held him to ground but he clawed the sealing mortification from his eyes. Cleansing light did blind him yet it also stimulated his imagination and inspired his Will. He ventures to rise. Failing he falters, he fails yet again, he hoards his endurance for renewed effort. The singers exhort him, they voice a chant of sanguine promise. The repetitive notes reverberate in the infested lump that is man without a Culture. A demand of resolution is prayered in beseechment of God. At last Western man decrees his ponderous self to be erect and he joins the singing with his detection of life's freedom.

And as the wilderness flowers so the West's summer is ephemeral. As the very apex is surmounted the gliding spirit of the Occident begins to arc over and slowly stretches in lateral descent to the forever solidness of the become. Death is consonant to living, the dark is of the end when the light is tapered to smoke. Exulted was the West in birth and boldly she now bids death to approach in unconcern. Europe shall not die in easement for it will be as if a mountain wombed statue is ripped out of the seams in demention and abhorrence.

Chapter 4

UNWRITTEN BUT APPARENT in the work of man is the awareness that endeavors and hopes are vainly damned unless higher purposes than survival and self-aggrandizement are fundamental. Little of worth has been painted onto the lens of history's lantern excepting that it be surpassing of prosaic acceptances. Some men have pledged their souls to loving life and by this insert into existence a security that obstructs fear's suspicion. And in the most difficult ages, by the strength of a tranquil spirit, an artist may be disclosed as of God in extracting prophetic insights that establish a belief in beauty as truth.

Man is a sacrificial ox set unchained but circumscribed on a river of disappointment. When he has equipped himself to navigate the mercurial shiftings of reality and is of experienced wisdom, he becomes bankrupt of response. For his body does sicken and perishes by aging. The emptiness called death does not fade, even if it is never echoed in the euphoric warmth that is tissue alive. Always there is the cognition that in all things there strains unlife. Vision ultimately confesses the inviolability of the last image that is of death.

Grandly in the end a discernment is shouted out as if a pirouetting trance. New life reasserts itself in a delight of fulfilling benevolences. How rapidly life vanishes and then it does return to lighten the grief number with its resurrection. Life ever vital does prosper over death. There are teachers, smitten with a fantasy of guilt, who preach the thought of death as an elegy to God. They find the Lord as their actuality and thus misinterpret the meaning of God who is the creator of existence.

God was first uncovered in the wet, chilled, magical

caverns of hunting clans. He had been the sky, the wind, the sun, the sea, and the sands, but not until his might had been structured in stone and wood idols, in charcoal shadings on cliff and cave wall, not until man coveted Him as matter in time was He discovered. The man who first captured God was a hunter, a warrior of the hills and of mountain footsteps. Along crevices frictioned apart by the earth's discharge of heat and mass, tiny groups of hunting folk took refreshment from the summer's drought and winter cold. They cultivated not but they had abdicated as fruit and nut rodents. For these early men were packs of shy predators. God was known only as a Cruelty, as a ferocious Entity who may protect if appeased properly. In expiation His beginning worshippers crushed the heads of their eldest on a master tree or upon the boulder squatted on the otherwise empty plain.

It is not difficult to understand the enshrinement by early man of the megalith. Tremendous shards of impervious matter, painfully flaked from open surfaced outcroppings, became man's primal Tabernacle. The monoblocks were man's introductory attempt to dissociate himself from animalistic totems. These monoliths waterclock a spirit as promising as that which proportioned Solomon's temple or Apollo's at Delos.

Before man was man there was nothing as a Culture. Aimless scourers of fallen acorns, eaters of the dead, wandered the unmarked terrain. Fangless, without velocity to make the pursuit, weak eyed matched to the falcon's surveillance, unarmored and lacking the ape's brawn, he wisely sutures endurance to his heart and lungs. With this tool created by Will he runs the lion to earth. Man is executive to the planet because of his hunger for safety and not conversely for omnipotence. He became man when he taught himself to strike a prey's neck with a stone. When he purposely caused fire he ended his consanguinity with the bear and attracted the dog. Forest man was innately weak and because of this he trained his skill of hand; succeeding in this he then began to sculpture himself. By compelling his inward horizons to change, man practiced the powers needed to construct cities as he confronted his jungle world. Without the hunter there could be no World History, without him God is alone for the hunter is man's father.

The West is not just this winter hailstorm, there was a spring concerto that begat the summer performance. Then comes the autumn sonata with a humility and eagerness that enters with distinction. In repudiating decline the autumnal West pours outrushings of creations into actuality. The Culture fought magnificently to avoid the inevitability and in challenging this predetermination she astonished history. This issue with death contended the moment's vehemence and extended its brevity.

The trees were tipped with fragile hue, the streets were lulled at day's close and European man exclaimed halt to the voracious chiming. Hints of decay were discernible in the tendrils of factory fume that served to outline the era's irresponsibility. Yet there was art and thought of magnitude in the same kernel of time.

An extended struggle commenced between surmounting life confronted with absolute decay. The West did not die easily, she battled organically and without pretense to buttress her walls against the sight of Cultural morphology. Savoring each denouement of the dawn, she intensely seduced the day. No Culture bristled at death with a greater confidence. The singers of the autumn episode were quite positive that they would defeat dying and the coming blackness with immortality. Nothing seemed impossible when poised to the ardent prowess of Europe. But as the exertions entered into the crucial stages, the West's blows became frantic. Europe's spirit was extenuated past recompense. It was then that she impaled her young men on the spikes of mechanized warfare. The dead thronged the pastures and soon the corpses inundated the cowbell and daisy.

During autumn Europe became an enchantress and did bewitch her own soul. This season of languid tincture was of a moment of exquisite productivity in all manner of art. If a demarcation would delineate the seasons, one might choose the year 1805 when summer expired. The day was of a sea battle off Trafalgar whence the period defaulted. A hundred cycles added and the difficulties of 1905 were reached. It was a frigid, rain laundered, morning when the Tzar's fleet was cannonaded off the Tsu-Shima islands. This is the instant when the denial of procreation was substantiated, when autumn lay victim and winter beared close ahead secreted in the thickening haze. It was a victory of Western technique and training over Western spirit. The West had allowed its very marrow to be lanced by her adopted child, Japan.

From the hemp rigging and yards of the Victory a course is made to the coal burning water machines of the Japanese navy. Gnarled, salt and sun bleached, hands pilot the English men-of-war into the battle line and into a century of excellence and decline. A greater weave could not have been suspected by those who worked the wooden ships. Voluminous explosions unconstrained sounded along with the cannon's injunctions. And in one hundred years the men of Nippon with English tutoring prepared the interlude's conclusion.

Beethoven is the instructor of autumn's pride. He is but one of many who spontaneously augment mankind's poem. In his groping for the deepening and serious explanations that all aware men seek, Beethoven chords the song of Cultural maturity. It is the artist's quest for fulfilment that shapes the ornamental flask that retains the Culture's inheritance. He and his brothers, Goethe and Tolstoy, bring to Western art ideas of incalculable pronouncement. Their predilection for man's spirit as eternally free conceives a Europe towering and indisposed to decline. Nevertheless it is a confidence mated with sorrow for an intuitive woe is found in the passages of sound and word. Always a threat of terrible danger exists. Of an infinity that is soulless and a sterility of life that is forewarned.

Russian musicians and writers drain the artesian wells of European art. Tchekov and Tchaikovski resolve the strands into unification. The impressive renditions of the eastern European artist contributes in goodly measure to the Culture. Beyond the Danube lies not Asia but Europe to Lake Baikal. Russia, by pulsating outwardly into the weakness of Asia, guarded the vineyards of France. At the gateways of Warsaw and St. Petersburg the surging Germanic music and thought found a sincere brotherhood. Russia is denounced as Oriental by jealous and fearful nationalists of the later Culture but such bias is ludicrous. For it is the Slavic novel, *The Idiot,* that vindicates the West as an entirety involved with a vision of man that is concerned with soul. Dostoyevsky portraits Europe as a land where harmony shall not exist as long as the society inflicts torture and death in an apparition of love and deliverance.

The idiot is Christ forlorned by time's forgetfulness. As he approaches winter his staked wounds are healed but blood profusely spurts from hidden wounds. Prince Myshkin is Christ of the West's autumn but his punctures are of his doing and not of any Roman. He is the West condemning itself for the reality of defeat. The idiot ravages his inner being of beauty because he can not consummate its need of actuality in a world that rejects gentleness and love.

Book IV

THE SOUL REMEMBERS

Chapter 1

MY INNER STRENGTH is fatigued by man's vicious conduct in this expiring century. Alone am I when my love toward mankind is absent, when I am a vacancy surrounded by wasteful hatings. Then I too forget how to love. Yet when swallowed to the dregs, my soul then confounds memories of sentient trust and tenderness. Cymbals continue to strike but those who hate are deaf to the appeal. Anxious fears clog minds and the body is disordered by the unseen revenge that engulfs the bitter men. Loneliness is prevalent and staring eyes are saucered with hunger for the symmetry of responsive love.

Exploring my self I strive for rapport with the world of my moment. I visualize peoples who fabricated chariots and ships where silt now pours over walls in wreckage. Hear the lost tides that once had cradled the giant surfing turtle. Taste the mud flecked waters of the Oxus where Alexander and his horsemen forded the stream. And thus my soul is aware of this beleaguered existence's auguries that do oracle tomorrow's concavity. In my plated spaces I am fearful of that morrow. All men who rush their intuitions down untrod roads fear the new beginnings that they help invoke.

Few are those who hear anything but the startled gasp-ings of their own irresolute Wills. Perhaps in a differing age they might have been amenable to tenacity's opportunities but in this day they are maddened by this hostile now. It is not possible to care for any premise of the winter world's attitudes, nothing is substantial except the facade. A derelict cynicism pervades even the child's playing yard and parents dread to speak aloud in natural instruction. The keepers of the concrete castles, incised so astringently by master Kafka, punish bolder spirits with the noose or harsher, embarrassment. But I shall write my insights into the brightest pause, for I am bidden to do this by my commission to the love of hope.

History is a watershed of rivers that aqueduct thru the netherlands of Egypt and Greece. It is a liquid wand of fact and myth, a torrent that is a sea avidly carried by creating life. World History is neither progressive nor cylindrical in effect. There are duplications in its currents but they are symbolic of existence and not of growth or repetition. Only planet earth is an organism of irrevocable growth, only her seasons are of Promethean recurrence. Mankind's history is the fullest bloom of earth's ontogeny. Man is not the child of the apes but of all matter's developments, of the motions in the sea and the abundance of the land. Man is fulcrumed by not only what he believes but by the circumstance of his society, thusly of his particular disposition in history's eddies. Winter man halters himself to the circled path of illogical progression out of desperation to find a placidity in this disconsolate nighting. The elimination of bodily disease rids not apprehension from the soul of man.

A Culture is a triumph for all men. We are animals and must not be shamed by this truth. History of this race is the smoke of combustioned sonnets and verse, of the reddened ghosts of running warriors. In the West's become she evades reality by printing profuse volumes describing the winter scene instead of crowding the juncture with feeling and art. Reconstructions of this winter episode are praiseworthy only when they establish the indisputability of Cultural oscillation. A poet of the early or mid-season is not concerned with compiling the details of his gropings in life, as he is addicted to the actual exploitation and investigation of his moment. History is dependent on reality, on adventures that support images of excitement.

A writer of commendation is aware of his ascendancy as an artist, as is the warrior who has conquered after a hard campaign. To be attuned to being is as the youth who finds love for the first time. To sense the presence of worlds now sintered gravel of the become is to live history. It is jubilation to be honored with intuitive imagination that allots the irretrievable to be as of this immediacy. Men, including the multitudes who claim no Culture, create by the act of disavowing fate a noble postulate. They do not have to bring significant material to man's tale if they, by personal example, hearten poets to lyricism. Proud is man though this winter impedes greatness for the dawns shall again be crisp and a thaw will be scented on the land.

Man's history is memory, individual and collective retention. Man issues his history although he feigns to forget the instant now. History is man's term for his comprehension of that selfish denial of life, death. Time exists for mankind's voyage on this planet but time is not of improvement or of series. What man mirages as progress is the space constricted ground leisurely revolving in complementary concert under his accelerated pace. Earth is factualized in time and space, man is not. His wending is loyal and enterprising but as time and space it is infinitesimal. Man's history is a poem of beauty and of tragic dignity.

History is a possibility for man only because he is proficient at retrospection. As a creature in solitude he remembers for terse intervals but as a race he hears the string harps and reed piping from the ice clotted seas of the past. History is the become held as inexact fantasia in man's mind, he lives as a being of remote yearnings and antecedents. Each individual birth is original yet also a continuation that withstands catastrophe. Writing, painting, sculpturing, and composing are the externalized resultants of inspirational remembrance and combination. The moment may well be stimulus to the act of creating but the propulsion had been fertilized in past engravings. Reason and discipline purify past and present into those legitimate impressions of art.

Man recalls the past in every exploit of the present even as the dialing shadow becomes a neuron in the subconscious. The enkindling hours of a hundred ages spent, thrive in today's man. Each primordial implosion is forever implanted in his being. Any man is a total cell of racial memory but with accentuations. The prodigious molecule that is earth serves as the breast of incipient acculturation. It is the same gland that feeds the naked stone thrower who trots the cloud starved dunes or the Greekling who cut the pantheon's frieze from the enslaved stone into a procession of clarioned life.

There are those who create history by their very act of movement. By their sagacity of precept and interpretation of fate they foil the age. Their donations to the society may be of protest as to the instant's vileness or a promptness of the period's enlargement. A man is born to an expansive Culture or to an ossified people of the become. The season can be late or early but a man's value to himself and his day shall always be eminent if his soul is braced with self-pride and determination. He is born amidst vandals and scavengers but if his sanctum of self-acceptance is not invaded by the heinous season he shall stand aside and be a dissenting Will. For in a day of improbity, nothing is as urgent excepting that man's potential of love and thoughtfulness to the future is actualized.

Chapter 2

ABSURDITY RAVAGES the age but there shall be those so garlanded with hope that they will oppose the ending and alter the river's bed if it be only a pebble's might. The newer movement may be ephemeral but it must also be real for all fluxed existence is enrichment to earth. If a man stands to test the bitter season, placing his position in jeopardy, then he is of royal stock though he is clerk or minister of state. Perhaps he is despised by his peers, a galley slave property to a pirate, a hair cutter on mean streets. What standing his birth or circumstance has given him is unimportant if his symbolic reality confronts his hour's spoilage. Man is of the enduring land and it has been and shall be again that there are those who show staunch idealism in the dimmest twilight.

Much is possible if man realizes that earth is his only exposition of life. Reproductive matter may be indicated at a far star system but this shall be rare. Planets in the unseen quadrants of space that rank with the fertility of earth shall indeed be unusual. Protoplasm capable of attaining the level of aware complexity that is man shall never be found unless man searches and finds himself. The universe is not quite as strange as the technicians of winter profound, and man is neither as diminutive nor as imperfect as man hating fanatics scold.

The universe is the ocean of wholeness as to matter, motion, time, and now is incomprehensible visualized separate from the mosaic that is earth. The planet is the creator of man and his histories. Earth and universe are as one in man's journeying yet they are not assimilable for the void is not of earth.

Yes, the marching of men shall at one moment or another be ended, man shall countenance defeat. History, memory is truer than facts for men act on impressions not objects, history is that which was once matter, motion, and time joined into an essence of past life. Each creation becomes a disaster of matter, disintegrated by uninvoked time. Surely it is cut into the mountain sides overlooking the caravan trails that rubbled hope returns in the next become to a newer prelude. Man is not everlasting, he too has a life tale as spring like and final as any Culture he procreates. In the confines of the limitless universe there is a hunger that earth does not contemplate. In that accomplishment of existence, the universe, man has intangible quality that candles the inanimate space. Man and vacancy battle for opposite goals. Man desires life, while the universe extends itself for the detonation of matter. Earth has produced a life immanence of originality, man.

Yet man is mortal and his swiftness is constantly braked by the accumulating friction of time. An age shall come when he will not recognize his history, that he, in years misplaced, was a warrior and a poet. As soul passes into a state of perfected concord it becomes a spirit of ash. Man is the destination of existence's formulations. It is his inner identity that prepares the cause and the result of his virtuosity as a living presence. Man shall die. The dying may not be of shape, he may revert, regress, to his infancy when a skill in plundering a bird's nest outpaced his embryonic soul.

By the term soul I mean to represent the ethereal repository of man's sentient awareness. Soul is the distillation of intuition and thought as men react to God and apperception. Soul is the mating of human resources, of mentality and of Will. There were life specimens who considered themselves to be the heir of earth, but their order in time as growth was unpropitious. Man must be sequent to the lava scourged brontosaurus. We are subject to what was actual beforehand as to that which we shall succeed to. An apparent progressive climb in human gain is rather the advancement and retreat that is indebted to planet earth. The soul of man is earth's cosmic revelation of life's creativity. Man was selected by the discriminatory earth to be an opportunity of elastic possibilities. He was a timorous fawn at his commencement but his brain led him into a confidence of life.

Essence is not an end or a birth, it is a condition of the moment that conceives and defines that instant's totality. The spirit of man is the being of earth but in the fracturing of winter the soul is reduced by futility and surrender. She is discomfitured and banished to inane discourses on I and I. However this climax of earth is stiffened iron, poured as molten fortitude in the wood smoked tunnels of apprenticed man. The soul of man is exaltation and is greater in effect than any of the exploding star novas that stun the universe, far out where space is too magnified to be sensed or understood. Where galaxies of suns burn in eruptions that toss swarms of energy across the flotation of emptiness. Where monstrous containers of matter are heaved for termless eons of time. All this immensity is diminished by man's soul.

By use of the word soul it is not to imply a contractual relationship to God or religion. Certainly in mankind's rationale an abstraction of the Lord as the precursor to religion did result; however, man's realization of God came after the soul was begat. Man resided on earth for a number of floods without the idea of God. Man was born as animal without a soul. Soul was derived in a protracted experimentation accompanied by purgative pain. No material benefit, no invention or technique, no bequeathal of scientific law or of the poet's lines can equal the enthralling art of man creating his soul.

By use of the word soul I chance confusion for the term is imbued with the odor of religiosity and of obfuscating theology. However, I can delve no other testimony better honed than this word's magical and inspirational dominion. Soul is the mother of each note composed by Mozart, of Marathon's Aeschylus, and of the Gods of Baal. Soul is the progeny of elemental man and that miraculous sensation of awareness revealed to earth by a stimulated soul, outer directed love. Man's rudimentary fact of soul was the love he gave unto a substance not of himself. The building blocks that enabled him to effectuate this deed were the aeons of laborious self-discovery that led man to esteem his own self. Loving is the soul free and membraned with myrtle.

In the society of the future sacred and refreshing love shall be subdued of its power because of ease of procurement. Man's soul shall be balanced and then men will begin to die as spirit. Outward love is disparate from animalistic protection, from mother warmth that instructs the guileless suckling on the method of survival. Between man's corporal and imponderable natures there occur clashes between fear and love. There is a synthesis of identification as the aftermath of defeat and triumph. Soul is reflex and response to conflict. Man enters the threshold of vision when poet and warrior combine to confer a self both purposeful and serene. It is of Cultural regression when attempts are made to resolve conflict by use of severe cathartics to induce an exiguous harmony.

Soul is far greater than that which is called ego, id, or libido. Soul is the total of the mind's thrust toward freedom as constrained and motivated by memories, intuitions, and judgments alien to all but man. Love is affirmation of creation, of procreation in song and city. It is the inner being of man that is known outwardly as the person. The estate of the soul specifies the detail and the indivisibility of the personality. If the soul is salutary and joyous in its precognition of life, so the entire man shall be. If the soul is apprehensive, suspecting, thus he shall remain unless a pursuit is prosecuted with resolution in finding interior light. As fire's battle of fear and love, so each soul indicates its intrinsic nature. Soul is the evening of conflict within the being. Soul is a daughter, it is love dampening hate and anguish.

Man has an inward way of life as relevant as the outer. Mystery and inspiration are the products of the interior struggle. The revival of earth by seasonal rotation sourced the conjurement that directed the soul into growth. Only the earth returns from the isolation of dying. All about, early man sighted death unrestricted as it pitilessly assailed living form. But the earth recants death each spring with voluntary life. A bewildered curiosity at the how of this infinite resurgence led man to a sense of propitiation and thankfulness. A gratefulness to reborn life eroded man's animal callousness.

To be a challenger to reality is to highlight that part of man's inner world which activates acute enterprises of soul and life. As a warrior may not escape the dialogue of combat, the soul too is of battle and it shall know death. A ship is alone in the rapacious stormings seeking solutions to constrict the uncontrollable. And as the ship is but driftwood to the winds, so the soul is not of consequences without the warrior's daring.

This moment is a become of adventures and of things memorable. This instant is mine and tormented though it be, I am jubilant in the joy of hope. I fear death not for its everlasting loneliness, or the silence, nor for the loss of the tangible and the soul. There are sad tidings but what is truly dreadful is the closure of the awareness of life, the stoppage of tomorrow's unknown. Adventure is the charm of life. Most can not be included in dramas of intense actions but all may march on the path of the mind's images and vision.

A person of inner trust desists from the acceptance of defeat. He possesses an invulnerable soul for it is undiminished by the daily availability of insult and degradation. It is the being who has faced the constant victories and defeats inherent to a commitment to reality whose soul is tempered and thus impervious to lasting surrender. Yet it comes to all men of any station or honour that at one time or another they shall turn traitor to their own soul. And it shall be that the individual alone will remerge the intactness.

My own conflict is brewed with a resolve of hope. I must, with inadequate knowledge and untrained sight, create beacons of word that inspire singing hope. Perhaps it will be rudely stencilled on a wooden post driven into a ridge of a vastness of grass that it was my responsibility to succor an infant from this aimless blizzard. That by loving life in a dreaded season I discovered a growth of indomitable hope in my soul and thusly in all men's souls. A hope that will be a palm tree to man, as indeed are the meager springs of the oasis to the Bedouin. Hope is an orphan of destiny and love. She is sturdy though bastard in parentage for hope is a surrender of faith that was once unshakeable and uninfringed. Hope is the last twig of the submerged forest that the misplaced stranger may cling to. Soul's most inner wall is the gift of hope.

My personal voyage is not taken on a sloop with iron cannon protruded over the roaming seas. Sailing with De Ruyter was not my dice's cast and I pull not the lanyard to salute the summer dawn. Sailing with Drake and Diaz, consorting with Prince Henry shall never be my duty. The Vikings were not my brothers and I am never of the genuine spring. To sail on a great cork of wood is not my moment for I tack only the ice clogged oceans of today. The battle of my season was titled Midway, a word ponderous with implication.

From the winter glacier a soft breath may be seen curled at the ice flow's edge. Youth of this snow canopied season have faith not in faith but in hope. Planet earth shall judge one last Culture of the sentient race, man. A momentous Culture waits in the seeded womb that is earth. Yes there shall be an affirmation, yes there shall be a coming creation of man. An intensity of new life bids her entrance, a new, old, God must be anointed. A reborn Apollo will swing the sky into a dancing. The seas shall be aflame with a woodland of torches lit by braving poets. Be patiently courageous and hold the course hard on the north star. Continue onward proudly and with nobility, have hope and a goodly tomorrow will lift from the sea's smoke.

This today is my only moment and I am its creature. To accept oneself as a man and then try to astound reality's parapets is the consequence of manhood. Turbid as this season is, it represents the only existence known to me. I dare not withdraw from it for with my escape I reduce myself to my soul. Worthy contests may only be played out in reality. A man must not live terrified, for he is satisfied only if he ignores the obloquy heaped on him by his fellow man and still stumbles forward. And if the air is infected with the effluvium of our flesh depleting technology, a man must stay to fight for beauty. To recede into the protection of passivity is to die.

Destiny is a thought born to few men and it weights them down with both impetuosity and a pretentious eminence. Perhaps it is my own fate to be regarded as a player of dirges. Yet I am a believer in tomorrow, in the beginning spring, in the resurrection of commitments to the future and to God. If I cherish the lingering of yesterday's potency, I also admit to the bestial conduct that proliferated in the most propitious of days. Listen in quiet to this warning I now exclaim. The become of this today I do dread for the dissolving West may erupt into a frenzy which could bring ruination to man as an entity with a history and a soul.

To this century of irrational custom belongs my verity. If imagination craves the rudder of a ship from Lysander's fleet, my imminence is of this day's momentum and coloration. A man never hides from his world's sun, and indeed if he decides, he can oppose the prevailing dismay.

Man is not easily divined, for is he not a contrary fellow?

He dashes to the constellations in delight, his soul is refreshed and the shackles of lassitude are detached. His spirit is free to lash and spin in gyrations steep and prolonged. Parabolas of glowing granulations mark his swath above remote earth. Man beholds a truth from this higher perspective, he is forever ignorant. There is in him an evacuation of learning as widely dimensioned as the blows off North Cape.

As long as man is perpetually ignorant he shall be young, aspiring to artless perceptions. Sadly, man can not remain this imperfect observer, and as the universe, he shall too become elderly.

All is irretrievable, man's desires have been entrapped in the deceptive canyons of reality. Notwithstanding, a better grip must be clasped, and then a plunge to continue the exertion. Finding inner resources, we hold the track. Treading in the heavy seas, we drench our strained lungs with sweet air. Afraid and erratic, we should persevere in seeking autonomy in the sinews of our hope. Tidings of our fateful miseducation should but excite our souls with questioning. If the fact of our inexperience is true, then man is a child with much left to be inquired of. To be aware of discovery is the joy of being, joy of becoming, and a festival of the soul.

Chapter 3

THIS MOMENT is my inheritance and it can not be deceived for I am a son of the winter moon. Although injured by debasements, one must wait in an assured manner readying the flare that forecasts the coming hope. America is my home, I have been fed from her honeyed breasts in all my days. My settlement in her realm is a pavilion of lush mead that is the continent's interior plain. My land on earth is a rich sea's bottom reclaimed by time. Plants wind exuberantly from the river and lake moistened soil. Even the Nile, when first plucked of harvest, was not greater than the generosity of my plain. Deposited in my land is a grandly sweet sea, a five fingered ocean with waters as unsalted as ever served the flocks of Abraham. Forests stalked to enormity, whose atmosphere is dampened mild by the uninhibited trees that boast their coverlets to the floating sky. My land was a cup of beauty, a calmness imminent of the mating of the morning tide. Vain warriors hunted the prairies with inbred stealth. Tree skinned craft of shallow draft glided over the earth diked lakes. Herds of deer and elk migrated the flats and undulations and these hunters were complacent not to be Gods.

The title New World is neither accurate in description or definition. Rather it was a New Europe that was established in the Americas and not a rudimentary world. An extension total both in effect and particulation was transferred to the Columbias from Europe. The United States beckoned as an extant promised land to the dissatisfied of a Europe that was becoming rigorously solidified. America was colonized by an adult society which negates those variables necessary to a new Cultural enactment. The diverse nationals entering the continent never banded into a racial people. They did, by dint of pragmatic compromise, brick a workable order similar in appearance to a crystalline mixture. The varied groupings kept their separate mores as sub-societies in the generally admixtured fluid. This order of solution could function well in the mechanical areas as economics, government, and defensive warfare.

America presents manifold dilemmas to the annotators of history. No state has reached the real or relative wealth as has the United States. And no nation with such material leverage has rejected the need to control world events excepting America. This presumed supremacy of Christian morality only conceals massive hemorrhaging of Cultural vitality and aggressiveness. America is an inseparable appendage of the European Culture and thus suffers from the morbidity of the young born elderly.

Woodrow Wilson and Theodore Roosevelt strenuously devoted their considerable mental and spiritual capacities to the hauling of their countrymen into the performance of leadership. These two presidents represented the best of the American ethos. In the period of a score of years these two attempted to stimulate the nation to aware responsibility of World History. The American people, being desirous of comfort and riches, rejected their better instincts. Wilson was the first American since the revolutionary Jefferson and Washington to approach the world scene as a projection of the American Will. The European masses were captivated by this great idealist and political teacher but his own American people had neither suffered sufficiently nor faced the agony of the soul's despair at mankind's brutality to accept his greatness. Roosevelt, though the recipient of an international peace prize, was eager to show the European powers that his nation had arrived in the scheme of things by insisting on increased naval armaments as indicated by Mahan. The Civil War had been too much glory and not enough a lesson. Domestically, only the Lincoln myth cast a questioning unease into the indolent miasma. A tragedy was effected when the Wilsonian concept of a United States of the world, as touched upon at the Hague Conferences, was ignored by the people of his own land. The League of Nations was debilitated before it became reality by the desertion of the American entity which at that point the world community did still trust. Probably nothing would have been changed for the trench war still would have been fought with its inhuman mechanizations and the economic stasis which followed still would have resulted, yet does not a grain of wheat signature hope to the famine stricken.

The American landscape of incredible diversification and beauty knows no method of birthing Cultural art and thought as expressed in form and science. She became an imposing figure to the world only after winter binds the West captive. Indeed there is a saffron wasting to this piping, for the American peasant as embodied by Lincoln and the pioneers was the bread that Cultures seek as sustenance.

The nation-state is not the resolution of a beneficent progression. The state of the West is a replacement of historically faulted kingdoms. As a people trains itself to regard sophistication and falsity as superior to simplicity, the kings die. Kingdoms are of spring and summer, as nations belong to climaxed autumn and winter gravity. Rome is of winter in all her moments excepting her rustic hours. The Latin spring was conducted in Athens and on Ionic shore, as was America's at Aachen and Pavia, and as Turkey's at Medina and Baghdad.

That Kant and Hegel should be inebriated by statism is not maljudgment but indicative of Cultural morphology. As savants they reside on the banks of their world's river and predict the becoming route. But as their role is rooted in summer, they see the future as a continuation of their own optimistic and healthful age, and not of an incalculable decline. These were masters of deductive and inductive reasoning, they were not impassioned and bewitched poets who believed in shadings and mists, not facts. Their consecration of the state apparatus anticipates Cultural putrescence. That philosophers could be persuaded of the efficiency of statism as the epitome of spectral progress is grotesque.

Mutations to presumably ingrained institutions presage the entire society as subject to organic decay. Bureaucracy and compartmentalization stand in the place of out of style loyalties, fidelity, and verity. In each Culture the older patterns are superseded as the slippage of the once resilient city is increased by a luxurious dependency to the state. Emperors and tyrants are promptly needed to rule the unruleable. These despots gild their tongues and hands in fulsome intent as they maneuver the mob, aristocratic or plebeian. Justice and mercy are lost in the contradictions of a society conventional in reply but diligently hostile to depreciated values. Still some few keep the flags safe from the adversity of disaster as they fight oppression not merely with actions but with the example of their own soul.

Alas, the day arrives when men of good will give all their faith to printed constitutions and decorous assembly. This urge for self-defeating regulatory guarantees is established to substitute for the decline of effective intra citizen management. Belief in the adroitness of form over style in government is the consequence of social contraction. Kings led Europe onto those vital roads of Cultural activation. Western drama had its list of principals headed by King Charles of Neustria.

There is a contiguity of fact transferable from Culture to Culture. And there is a rhythm of response that appears in the communities of man. And there is wilderness, spaces not of man. Fertile delta or wasteland, there is always an unknown earth to be domesticated. And from the forest tracks, from the sheltered glade in scape of rock, from wind mothered sands comes the warrior-king. At his initial testing he is the master hunter, then a patriarchal captain. His nature may be unpleasant but this is unimportant for nothing matters except his prowess in the hunt and in war. And though he be wicked, let his bravery be fierce and his sons shall be royal.

See now the stinks bellow, a world sunk in the refuse of industrial secretment. The beaver's pond is loathsome to the taste yet bad water is the only reservoir to quench the thirst of living, of respiration. The goodly waters are covered with the pale greenness of death. Valleys of uncrested stumps that were the hunting grounds of the Franks today are ill-defined cemeteries for hundreds of thousands of unremembered rifle men. Today where the mucous, the rancid waste of the necropolis, touches, it brings harm. Prickly brush land where once young serf and Duke watched the updrafted falcon peregrine soar are in this now burial plots of untried hopes.

In the beginnings there was blood, a great excess of it, but legends were issued along with the grievous wounds. The fleetest of the hunt founded warrior tribes and from these the boldest sired kings. Yet savages build not Cultures. For this rising of the soul needs stonemasons and narrative troubadours. And such men were adapted but slowly from the tumultuous pages displayed by the indistinct kingdoms.

Book V

NOW THE POTTER'S WHEEL

Chapter 1

ATOMIC ENERGY delivers to man those powers previously consigned to the universe. Man has an appetite for tools of such character that they would enable him to rid himself of those frailties of his animal origins. There is in man a dissatisfaction with his physical ineffectiveness as matched to his precincts. He wished to surpass in size and strength those giant vertebras he pursued.

His genesis as a limited physical factor forced him to chase as a pack. Handicapped by his size, he fitfully assents to the development of the family intactness. It became to the mate's advantage to stay with the female and her brood past the nursing period needed to safeguard the infants. He was inadequate to survive without her and the children's help. Man engaged a protective love for family only as a consequence of his animal need to add to the pack's cohesiveness as a hunting unit. As the lion hunts in prides and as the elephant herds close in to sleep, so man thrived as he joined into the groupings that still presumed not to be a mankind. Between man as a hunter and other carnivores there exist fundamental distinctions. All but men are intrinsically self-contained hunters. Man without weapons of the simplest stone missile or stick club can not compete as a predator.

A species of life may be too successful on the ecological scale. The saber-toothed tiger and the mammoth are in no way inferior to today's Bengal tiger or the African elephant, except as their slighter brothers have persisted. It is in their very biological superiority that one must seek the reason for these life form's vanishments. Unquestionably each of the giant felines daily hunted a large territory making it eventually bare of game, thus his success in bulk achievement destroyed him. Not able to subsist on fruit, grass, or insect hive, he had to kill quantities of fresh prey each day in order to maintain his minimal needs. Awakening before sundown, he would begin his nightly ranging in further and further travels. And then the moon would rise when he no longer could continue the chase.

The mammoth also was destroyed by hyper success. Wonder at the tons of foliage needed to sustain the mighty herds for but one week's movement. And if these animals are like their smaller descendants, who prefer young saplings for the bulk of their diet, then the mammoth's problem is only more so difficult. As the centuries ringed the living tree and the leafed branches remaining each spring were higher on the trunk, these beasts despaired of existence. With each new day came demands of exertions impossible and living became unrewarding. Their own animal properties victimized the behemoths. As stalagmites bulge with aging's droppings, it is the oceans of earth that can support the greater breeds. The buoyancy of salted waters and the richness of its nutritious chemistry still provides a recompensing world for the blues and sperms.

The devolution of past zoological periods in most instances was the culmination of physiological and anatomic gargantuism. Hulking reptiles were slain by their own success as biological overgrowth. The dinosaurs were perfectionists in converting plant food into flesh and bone. Their bodies became monuments to overconsumption. This Pyrrhic victory recoiled to thwart the lizard for not only did grazing become problematical, they were also too ponderous to speed to safety from the floods and fires common to their habitation. Obese they were and thus could not finish the race to food and future.

Earth is a place of exotic and fermenting life. She alone is a miracle of fertility, for earth is the hatchery of living matter. It is the entire history of earth as time, space, and matter in motion that is responsible for sentient organisms prevailing over physical giantism. Earth motored the pulse of being and then this living substance pollinated a spirit, a soul, which is mankind.

Once there was a space of long, long, time on this earth

when the unfolding of things alive was invigorated by the exhibition of fertility as a stipulation of environment. The improbable lakes of oil and beds of coal that lay underneath the crust of earth presuppose an animal and plant plenitude in abundances of multiplying forms. Thusly the transience of archaic ages was caused by excessive propagation and cellular corpulence. Life is exuberant to the dimmest of species and any living cell will coronet emphatically for unconstrained proliferation.

Perhaps man in today's imbalance of soul prefers a reptilian death. Unspoken requests for the grave have been latent in many of man's chapters. The scale swings to either side and thus the plummeting of numbers during the Roman winter was not a fact of palpable desolation or aftermath of erratic surplus but rather was a disinclination to continue the procession of life as the Roman spirit had become exhausted.

In the transposition of the mind's picturizations into the writings that appear on this page an indeterminate measure of meaning is left inert in the air. I repeatedly stress the thought that the relationships between historical eras are definable and not consanguineous. Innumerable facts and tools do find felicitous passage, however. Cultures are distinctive in spirit, art, and attitudes. In an absurdity to prove a benign progression to man's story, historians elude the obvious and place in prominence those happenings that suggest general connections between alien worlds. In the quest for explanations to fatalities of epochs, these scholars add to the delirium that all moments are similar, and that man is indistinguishable in all seasons.

The resurgence of the Iberian peoples during the Moorish occupation is a significant example of the exhilarating reserves of Will accorded to a Culture in robust health. Spain though in bondage to a mature Culture chimes the European melody of springtime. The Spanish military and dynastic majority of Europe's summer is due in some extent to the techniques adopted in the Cultural contention and transference between the Arabian and European worlds. But above all else, beyond the gold of the Americas, Spain was crucibled by the quality of spirit that drove her sons to explore the horizons. In combating the Caliphs Western enterprise was intensified in the Spaniard. Conflict implements maturity and Spain, by waging war against the Magian civilization, cemented in herself an unparalleled scope and vigor in conquest and expansion.

A philosopher instructed in the Greek or German conventions of logic returns to essential answers of form and structure that are interchangeable in any world. Logic is a technique of the prepared intellect. The competence of the mind's dialectic mechanism produces equivalent roads thru the puzzles of man's cognitive executions. As if copied intact from age to age are those restrictions regarding religious and moral procedures. Morality and guilt are implements of the soul exercised in reality as the conscience responds to disturbing activities in the social complexion. Unfortunately the tools of social jurisdiction are wielded in fear and distrust instead of compassion. As a society's temper weakens, so its rigidness toward class and sexual censures modify. Laws to limit desires and lusts are inscribed in every society's commandments and are transferable from moment to moment. Punishments will vary drastically in manner but still not effectively.

As one tries to perceive the meaning of World History, there is an admission that a progression of materialism and technique does exist. There is an accumulation of tool and fact stored in the records and the manifestations due reality. Education is the collector of the past retentions of matter control. Knowledge as opposed to intuition and insight is reproducible from century to century. This accruement of fact, whether it be legal codification or of agronomy, states a perpetual additionaling to man's bank of fact. Predicaments of existence are present in all social organizations and the utility of technical transference is understandable for man demands a securely constructed den.

Change is abhorred in any society after that order has learned to fulfil its members' needs in practicalities and also as a fortress from danger without. Today tiny tribes of primitive folk still birth and die as excluded beings apart from the concourse of man. The remoteness of their homes prevented intimacy with any worlds but their own constricted tribal arrangements. Transference of technique can take place only when each partner is sufficiently willing to accept the other's potency. When offers of fact are embraced by the primitives often an accelerating debilitation takes place, most discernible in costuming and food and beverage intake. Man is a promiscuous hardy who is attractive in growth, as are youthful Cultures who assimilate complexities of tool and fact from strange worlds without surrendering a tithe of originality.

If all the peoples of earth had been born to sheltered vales where sufficient food was available through the centuries without laborious cultivation, then man would have been always a careful fellow of secure habits. Wars, floods, or any upheaval incite changes that are followed by renewed effort unless they are caught in Toynbeean rout which overwhelms the entity. Famines chased a host of warrior tribes to the investigation of the mountain's far side. Disaster is the prelude to the reformation of experience, while if stability nipples contented animals it also removes adventure and poetry from man's soul.

Exchange of fact has not to do with the spirit of the soul or the spontaneity of art. A flint is handed from age to age with improvements made constantly to the tool and still it is an identical spark that is released. Yet the issued light unveils divergent symbols in each era.

The world is a composite of man's experience, while the earth is a gift of the Lord's universe. In a season of sophism some courage is required to exclaim of the Entity who has brought life into the mud of impenetrable time. He is Thee who created the become from which awareness descended. The universe has custody of matter that is of life. Extraordinary varieties of lesser cellular organisms await discovery but this future denouncement is a light year of ages remote. This wilderness on earth must be diagrammed before man can imprison the greater unknown.

Facts are accrueable, they are amassed on the concrete technology of human activity. A fishing hook of green sapling is of heritage old, and man is competent of instruction from the become, from the ever expanding past. A legacy of historical empiricism is communicated from generation to generation. The accumulation of tools does benefit the newest, rather oldest man, as a physical component of actuality. Many facts are lost but faint clues do lead to the unearthing of predecessor crafts and their manufactures.

This Western winter secludes herself behind an impostor's decoration. The autumn harvest is dissipated and man distorts his features as he views his silvered self. He hopes still to find a perfected society in the reflection of his prismatic aspects. The soul is not the provider of social orders. Despondency invades the soul of man as this instant is barren of faith's fidelity. Hear the winds encumbered with the thin squeals of the demented strawmen. The ending West is a labyrinth of hallucinations and destiny has unseated the dawning.

Chapter 2

THIS EARTH, THIS HOME land to all man, has annexed the handsomest of compensations from the fates. She has induced mankind to be her son and he in reciprocation contributes the creation of Cultures to her being. A Culture makes entrance when the psyche of a people is enceinte with memories of a comradeship of goals. They are united by revelations of extraordinary hopes.

There was a time when Europeans of good will believed a society of ideals and sanity would follow the kingdoms as a matter of natural law, as progression. This dream of an enlightened world does not culminate this West. Massed schooling was the placebo that benevolent men pledged the future serenity to. Lamentably, runaway societies can not be haltered by the dissemination of fact. Knowledge is useful only when it is coalesced with Will and spirit. It harms not to teach the peon that the stars are gigantic bubbles of forever gaseous materializations. Yet was it foolish that he once thought those speckled flickerings to be tears that were strung across the firmament to ransom the darkness with awarenesses of love and pity.

Christ is the riddle of the European soul. How is it explainable that this teacher of the Greek winter participates in the West's ethos of aggressive aggrandizement? What gentleness in man confesses the legend of a Messiah saving men from damnation to be songed throughout the most cancerous of ages? Why is His unauthenticated memory loved by jealous and competing peoples for a score of centuries?

That Christ lives, though subdued, in this day of torture and rage is evidence that hope and love are competent forces to rival hate and fear. Today His name is an indistinct message that answers the anguished need for an inclusive expectation. That He did or did not live is inconsequential, and that He performed fine miracles is only transitorily meritorious. But that Christ infuses but a few souls with compassion in this very hour is of astounding distinction for every man.

This Messiah without credentials forever demonstrates that love is not of nature but is an extension of man's need for a meaning transcending recordable facts. This facet of man divides the bodily functions and frailties by uplifting the spirit into acceptance of God and death. Man is the arena between soul and animal and if he is removed of either contestant he becomes an insufficient spigot to his fates. Love is the progenitor of a wafting humana that calls men away from debasement and profligation. Christ is indicated to men epochs before His birth. His deliverance was forecast in prophetic utterances whose commanders knew not the wheel or the bronze blade. For Christ is the soul of man earnestly seeking a solution to the dissensions of animal rage. Christ is the historic key to man's insolvable enigma as to the personification of the Lord. He is the ultimate symbol of mankind's homoiousia with God, proof that every man can be the son of God. He is a bride of the animal and soul that lattices man to the Lord.

Man despises to think of himself as a predator. Yet the croon of the species is of unrelenting fratricide banked by animalistic jealousy and greed. Man has not achieved a contented, reproductive, or creative society. As earth has a planetary history and man a life specimen history, so both are intertwined in becomes, nows, and becomings. Man has reached his physical and mental possibilities but contrary to the planet he has not entered a reconcilable and consistent state.

After the dissolution of the West a World Culture shall ensue, and when that newer entity dissolves, an age of civilization shall be on man. A perfected society will come to prevail. At this confluence both artistic and Cultural creation shall be fossil. Man, to inherit more than a dash of ephemeral glow, will be coerced to curb his extravagant nature and cease to be poet and warrior. A satisfaction is to be displayed with the World Culture. When this is ended he shall never again thrust a Cultural hymen. Man will mineralize into a total civilization, a civilized dome that prohibits spontaneity and is rejective of aggression as contemptible.

Christ is a purification that consumes the Athenian world in its fire. Christ then is a delineated notch in history's displacement. He is an original Being in the annals and with His journey an emphatic fissure occurs in human affairs. Christ is the vase that incorporates man's contemplations for all the time before Him.

Muted whistles foretell novitiate ideas as revealed by surging Will. The fact of Christ's spirit is the mystery that overawes his observable actualization. For if Jesus was not the Christ, if the Messiah was ten different men, if He was an Essene founder, if he never existed except as a hope in the Hebrew underprivileged, none of these unknown factors are of momentous implication placed against the truth that Christ's passion was assented as truth. His becoming was not registered but he commends men in recompense for their growing soul. Inquiry and disputation as to His verity as child to the Lord and Virgin is speculation. But that He responded to the pleas of a dismayed humanity and did bathe them in love is of the soul's ingathering.

There is not a regulatory improvement in man's story. Centuries of material betterment fail in a season's complacency. If there is neither a repetitive circuit nor a progress in man's opera, how and where is a Christ placed in the strings of man's harp?

Along side the history of earth, of Cultures, of animal man, is there furthermore a chord of man as a beholder of soul?

Yes, history as growth perseveres as to the inward receptacle of man. A flowering soul is traceable throughout the archives of depreciated worlds. There is no superman awaiting the voyage's end. Our ship is earth and she is a vastness unmatched in hoisting excellent adventure. A greater man is not required for we are the superior man and have lived some six thousand years of Cultural elaboration. What gave a minted stamp to the supermen was the discipline of a purposeful soul. That a classification of living matter could be aware of art is astounding but it is surpassed when it is inscrolled that man also created a soul competent of loving God. All the Christs of the ages, saints, martyrs, and prophets are the protracted reality of soul victorious over animal hate and greed. Is it necessary to remark that soul is not a constant condition and that it is subject to the dictums of growth so it also may suffer decay, and that the health of soul is deeply affected by the season, to be harmonious or nihilistic.

Man's capacity is shared by his dual nature. Animal man has an attunement to life and death that soul man can not comprehend. A Christ becomes divested of animal man's failure to abate his appetites. Regardless, this animal who masticates his competitor is the father of kings and poets. And be informed that the eventual conquest of soul over disharmonious passion precludes that the last artist shall be still born.

Future ages shall not behold a superior type of man. Present man is the apex of earthly abundances. This race shall not graduate into a better breed, we will not birth genius by selectivity. Genetic controls may procure a refined intellect but this determinable hybridization is a double axed commission. A higher degree of mental aptitude in no way insures a better species. Soul has no intellectual equations, for insight, intuition, and creative purpose are not arbitrarily concomitant with intelligence.

To breed away masculine arrogance for replacement by an exceptional but unincisive intellect represents self-emasculation. Art is the creation of awareness muscled by a replenishing Will. Mental multiplications do not conclude finer poets and scientists. Creators depend not solely on their cogitative ability but more so on methods of extrapolating symbols from a filtered totality. Empathy and judgment are not simply extrusions born from experience and intelligence. These jeweled crowns can be attained by various routes. These are the first requirements of genius; a thirst to know, to seek truth, and to explore.

Chapter 3

THAT THE SOUL shall dial a passivity to man's passion has no explanations for this volatile season. If a man is to be of courage, he is energetic with animal blood. To build a Hagia Sophia or a Thutmose's tomb confers a boldness of intent. Chastened earth has foaled a being that is both violently extreme in procedures and is also of a communion with awareness. Soul, when exacted totally, is the become of man.

Mankind has a springtime and a winter, seasons to glow with life and midnights to shrivel in death's ebb tide. And the coming World Culture shall pronounce that inventive energy still rides in the gonads of man.

This severe present is of qualitative virtue for in its harsh challenge it sponsors great countering determinations. There is not a consecutive advancement in World History but there are contours undeniable and inflexible. The quiescence of the past is of discernible ripples. Those who speed with the need of exclamating freedom that unlocks life from its inevitability, who sense in each brief instant that we are beings alive, they too shall slip the knots to the wharf of life. And thee shall float adrift till the sea swirls the solemn form to oblivion. Man is not rock but wild winds of feeling and of hope.

I dread those seizures of nihilism that are a part of man's character for in every human there are the not obscure teeth of a meat tearing canine. Hate is a stipulation of the predators' existence. Heinous fury that admits a child perishing from a molestation. Aberrant misconduct may be found in any man. Habitually it is the lack of psychic balance that results in criminal baseness and not biological defect. When man was in the jungle fronds before there was an order of any form, he ate his young if the need arose. His brain's composition was already perfected in the forest but soul was not separated from the gluttony of earliest man.

His jaws were strong and equal to reach the bone's juices. He was alert with fear as habit that sped him from real and unproven peril. He was the homo of the woodlands without a soul. A beasty was he that could not be nominated as man. With no soul he was at best an animal with intelligence. Soul is inbred but not instinctive. It, as the essence of man's faith, shall bring peace to humanity. Soul is at the least an automatic responsibility for one's acts and goals that precede from a strenuous endeavor to accomplish goodness and truthfulness. Empathic love, which is the dynamics of the soul, is the single feature of our race that is of regenerative improvement throughout periods of horrendous reaction. Man, hesitant and stumbling, grapples with his several selves for an illimitable symmetry.

Man is as the kelp of the sea's surface, abright at night, but quickly defeated by the influence of earth that takes all down into the sunken places of her crust. It is a hurting thing to confess that we are neither immortal nor rewarded with ultimate salvation. Only life of the simplest cellular rendition is given the full trial of the ages to cavort in unheeding fecundity. Men are products of a nonrecurring cycle, a no cycle. We attend life as a season of spontaneous growth that has an extinction in the viability of reality. Cultures are the loftiest contribution that we have created and man is earth's most proficient species of adaptability. Man is the beaming that confronts the nugatory space. We are not the stock that is of the galaxies, we are their emissions. Severe as a young planet, earth in time became a courtesy of magnanimity that nursed the quiver of life that man is. Bellicose ice ridges scraped the land clear of protocasts in the preparation of the land for man's Culture.

Man was only furnished with life's breath in the autumn of planetary history. Two parts of earth's three have been opened before men are provided with existence. He enters a season of comparatively tender rains and warmth from a tamed sun. Tens of millions of yearly vegetations have provisioned a zone of atmosphere to hatch his fragile life. It is of concern to pry from indistinct time a photograph of this three placed planet of the sun's matriarchy. A canvas of exhaustive exquisiteness would have to be brushed to realize this orb of seas. Man traverses the age of space untutored and he arrows the density of the never mapped with emotion. In mankind a crescendo is orchestrated with a tonality that disregards indefatigable death. Eventually the soul's aria shall delight even the autonomous oceans.

Soul is the rejoinder to the necessity of rest, of a finality to animal libido. There is an echo to all that is suffered. Tragedy is man, for his soul, even as it blooms, shall toll end to the escapade. We will be organized and controlled inwardly by an extensive quality of justice. Man's adventuresome pose shall be as the defenseless isle after a tidal wave. Poets and hunters never will step the morning's passageway. Rigorous obedience will clog the orbs of the animal. Impetuous pride that had been the foundation of the city shall be forfeited. In the days of civilization that follow on the World Culture man will be calmly patient, he will never again seek boldness of action.

This Western submission of now is of eventful fermentation. From this interment a re-creation of the world shall be pleated. The new Culture will be as regal as the redwood that curtsey seldom to the sovereignty of Aethra. It shall be a Culture of solace and isolation as compared to the disheveled and erratic peoples of yesteryear. Men, those of the Yangtze and those of the Colorado, will be one tribe and there will be but one kingdom and one Deity.

Pain and torment are the hooks of the Arctic sea and man must sail o'er all the oceans. To suffer is to be of life, to be born of affliction and hope is of being. To be discarded by death in one of her varied modes is but a fluttered sobbing of destiny to the builders of twig and sand castles. To be man and not to be loved but demonstrates to the poet that he must love ever more tenaciously. To be qualified of loving one should be examined by failure. Nothing meaningful is won by the uninvolving coincidences of birth's good fortune. Every king is an unraveled screen of images to be defaced or idolized by the wavering shadows. A moment of living is to be cherished. It is a marvel when man becomes conscious that he is of living stuff. To see the yellowed glint of sun play with the greens of tree and field is of an elation that ducklings feel when first they depart the linn's gleaming. A swift hour to inquire at the bowed immensity of sky and a second's beat to wonder at the blue and white elegance of the rotating heavens. This hand that folds itself to the pen is my fact of awareness. The gift of sight is of a monarch's scepter. To watch the lithe trout approach the dusk from a pool's blackness is a fine association to life. To pace a field rutted with wagon path, face and palm stained with picked berry, is a goodly awareness of living.

Man is but a wolverine with a sometimes soul. He has impaired his life's harmony with distrust. The summation of his record of self-enlightenment is the weather planed face and poverty ravaged hands and neck of a bereaved fellaheen woman. It is not faith or hope that has kept man from prescriptive suicide but rather those instantaneous recallings when he was aware that he was alive with living.

Beloved children are protected from reality, apart from their homage to growth. Ignorant of dying and anguish, their entire world is of life, but not of actuality. Children's souls are seedlings but in their gracious state of untainted blossom they are of a far grander dimension than a propitiating temple on a seacoast's inlet. The children of men are the essence of spirit yet they create not even awkward water jugs. They create only selves.

Book VI

THE AIR AFIRED

Chapter 1

TO SAY IS NOT TO DO but words do indicate prejudices. And if a thing is constantly uttered with dramatic inflections, it may gravitate to the act performed. A discourse directed to historical prevision may endanger reality causally. Thus what ensues is wrested from me in hopes of not provoking disaster but by revealment to prevent abhorrent deeds. Nuclear fission is a fright heretofore undivulged. Never has man had such a solution to his social and animal frustrations. Thermonuclear warfare portrays a forbidding conclusion to mankind's perplexities. It would be audible admission that his experimentations with social combinations have been absurdities of matter and spirit.

Emphatically there is a foetused Culture slumbering in the earth's loam. However there first may be a cataclysm denuding the planet of form. Thusly I state that it is likely that this staticism of the West shall be extinguished by atomic fire. Hence, the Cultural cities of Europe will be blistered with dust, the concrete spans and steel beams that grid the world will be a fused mass. All shall be incinerated, the schools, the Houses of God, yes the children of man shall be devoured by the air afired. The museum vaults will be split apart and the manuscripts of Beethoven will be but meager tinder to the inferno. All that is earthly man, even if it be a conservatory from wickedness, shall not be omitted from the conflagration. How silent then shall be the burning cities. Withering as this end action of the West shall be and as pitiless as the winds of fire will be, all will be healed. Indeed the land shall throw off its lingering malediction and man will return in a re-mating that encourages faith.

The weeping shall be only of an interlude as the few survivors shall have many difficult feats to enact. The remaining literal world will be of doubtful appraisal. Perhaps the Ronsevaux of the unsophisticated and erstwhile West shall be retold. In this bleat of winter there is a paucity of courage and grandeur remembered. A decaying Culture has no need of heroes, as it has not the steadfastness for smallish imitations of Augean efforts. Where are the Wills of the West, for without them an infirmity is certain. No technique of law or tool can save this suspicious world from the throes of her deteriorated spirit.

Am I a furtive hater of man, am I a demon that savors death? In my aberrations do I harm a world I can not adjust to? Is it that I am but one more uncertified and spurious verbosity in an era of sophistry? Is it in my own Plantagenet phantoms that I mistakenly behold the future? Am I a destructive personality who needs to damage that which is alive including my own soul?

There have been prophets who sailed the seas of transcending awareness. Alas there has not been an assertive seer for many a century. Thusly how dare I divulge thoughts dreadful regarding the children of man. If I am disordered perhaps I see reflections of history as if they were but objects of some psychotic disturbance. Yet I shall continue to meditate aloud on this moment of alarm, on this present betrayal of life.

A moan is murmured but it is a cry of a mute as the ears that were to catch the appeal are burnt off the raw skull by the roaring bombs. Any book is papered scrap to the flames, even the rarest papyrus of magic. There shall be no coolness to float upon in the thicketed brook for the trees fiery feed onto themselves. Nowhere is there safety from the missiles, the grossly exaggerated slugs of the hunter.

History does have an ending cadenza terrific with false revelry. A dot in time that connotes the last vibration to living current. There are no guarantees that the bombs will not eradicate the regulatory life systems of earth needed by man.

This sequel must be reversed for life does renew itself, and though a season of ice may prolong itself ten thousand summers, one warmish noon a spring shall come anon. From the fire's residue a resurgence shall breast dense forests. Have conviction in growth as life, the alive instant of the may fly. Trust layers deep in Antarctic chill the crustacean that sucks life from the mud.

The frenzied groans of the necropolis shall be silenced by the flames. The planet's urban areas shall fall victim to the fire storms that will toss and twist across a prostrate earth. All peoples will be included in the West's ruin. Places of remarkable history shall burn as well as the inconsequential parish town. Wild grasses will be poisoned and the herds shall dwindle. Incalculable is the extent of the coming horror. It shall be as if God Himself took up the sword and slew the world.

It is with dismay that I persist to write of this nightmare. There seems to be a need for self-annihilation that lurks in the resignation of the West. Europe is trapped in a melancholiac depression. A futility and a caustic disbelief in ideals, faith, and archetypes is apparent as viewed in the languid art of winter. Two extenuated branches of concerned literature express the morose lot of this Culture's winding ribbons.

Astonishing words that describe unheroic, caged, men who insist on remaining true to ideals of heroism. Characterizations that present man's individual efforts to ennoble himself as in contrast to the demeaning and degrading season. The stories and novels by Hemingway and Sholokhov accent this class of writings.

The deputy class of responsible literature is of recantations that symbolize the deterioration of social anatomy and intrapersonal contact. From Proust and Joyce through guidepost Kafka a reckless discipline is exhaled in anticipation and analysis of the season's disemboweling fraudulency.

A pseudo recovery has emerged from the wars of this century. From the American middle-class and the European peasantry's tenacious resiliency the resources for this material revival were mined. These strongholds of stability gave a charade of continuity to the world after the downfall of Hitler. Western technical competence projected a filter of industrial wealth to hide the disorientation of a dying Culture.

European man is compulsed to be concluded as an entity. He desires a season to gorge at omnipotent glands, a morning to skip unconcernedly down the poplar groves and the stretching river. There is a time to sow the wheat and an hour to fulfil a woman's immediacy. And there is that lonesome moment of death. That wavering of the rye stalk, when at once in that identical possession of the clock's tick there is pain, fear, hope, and then rushingly a quietness that is perpetuated to the become's end.

That the West dies makes explicit the truth that she lived and crested history's milling narrows. Today the Culture is threatened with climax but this is a reality of man and is consistent with all organic adventure. Europe begged the Gods for relinquishment from her infected body. There is also an hour when to be alive is no longer a tribute to destiny.

The West shall not recede into an age of civilization. How incredible it would be if this Faustian Culture could transform herself into a pageant of Caesars and empire. With dedication I implore for that meeker bitterness of tyranny. Yet I know my premonition of calamity is not erring. The expenditures of the West's Will shall be unclaimed in her culminating paroxysm. All that is gluttonously pursued as wealth by the strawmen shall be no more. The turbulent hive cities and their masturbated suburbs shall be no more. The technological fungus will be molt to the fire storms.

Inundated by the Herculean appeal of Western power the crippled civilization of the East encased itself in the girdle of modernity. These peoples were summoned from their passivity by the European incursions. A style of resigned forbearance was agitated by the passion to throw off the intruders and yet to partake in the West's technical progress. Like those primitives who are brusquely jerked from contentment to greeds of strange stimulations, a pattern of exaggerated hope is hallucinated in spirit and actions. With tremulous palpitation Asia clutched the prancing West to her and in animalistic heat began to gnaw at the new matter. By this carnality the ancestral modes were shed and the soul of Asia began to change. Stimulating delusions came to those of the Tigris and the Ganges. In older times these peoples had been potentates and now again the West had traumatized their reality's inertness into invigorated force and Will. Asia reveled in the power of the new technology but she was deluded. Her viscera became ill and soon she joined the West in the prevalent insanity. The Orient and Africa came determined to share in Europe's sorcery and thus they shall perish with the West.

It shall come to pass that the patina of man's six Cultures shall be ash, of less weight than a drone's wing. Living things will no longer wander where once their elan surmounted the lofting condors. The cosmos writes not mankind's doom but chiseled into the shore boulders is the insistent stanza that brilliance and disaster are entwined in one vine. This essay is fitted not to interject despondency but to forewarn man with the drifting of the season.

There shall be a fine Culture to be applauded after the flames have subsided. But worldly man will be slaughtered, nowhere in the crushed pits shall a response be voiced. Perhaps in the earth's recesses and crevasses a reduced humanity will love women and the hunt. The technologically green towns will not preserve men for they as their monstrous offspring shall be less than dust. Not the university communities freaked with elephantine dropsy, they shall be less than the dust of dust. Not safe are the humbler nations, who effort to tunnel their presence away from the menace, for their avidity for station's power will be dust. Over the entire planet only a few sites shall be secure from the choking flame. A race of seven billions is to be diminished to less than fifty millions. This ragged covey will suffice for with their memories they shall cleave the earth for a preparatory spring. Savage peoples will add not their ranks to the spared for by the night of the flames these stone age men shall be ensconced in the cities.

I perceive that the blackness of the bonfires shall come in the first decades of the next century, or sooner. A tyrant, for only dictators will rule by then, of one of the supernations shall hurl a nuclear spear in a frustrating abortion of hope. Traduced into the madness, perhaps by a smaller state, the huger nations will bombard the planet with thousands of fusioned darts.

Yet behold, from this bewilderment a spring alluring shall be liberated from the carbonized earth. A verdure shall envelop the seared planet with libations of growth. And man shall be a forest of life with the sulphurated ulcers healed. Tiny patches of uncauterized land will provide for the bands of families dotted about on the earth's dryness. Not in Asia or Central America's tight spiral shall man remain and not in any square or angle of the West's major domains shall he exist to climb from out the furnaces that swelter the soil itself. Only in the technological world's least desirable places shall man begin anew his march.

To the fallow expanses he will return as a oneness. Man will come back to the idled harbours and sail out to hail the sea. This Culture will be one nation, one tribe whose fathers were consecrated by the flames of devastation. They shall be the race of heart and gusto. At the River Nile the men will find a solace that encourages a declaration of restored life.

Chapter 2

I HAVE SPOKEN of Will before, that inner radiance that goads the limbless to crawl. Hate and fear are the ghouls that expel the light. When a man hates, he lusts to do murder. To be destructive is to satisfy in man that which is the animal luxuriating in madness. Cultural fatigue and breakdown produce the syndrome of destruction. Every being is affected by Cultural decline on a personally psychological level. No man is ever an island and in the raging winter this becomes the litany for surviving egos. In this hiatus before retribution I publish my manifesto in hopes that it will be brought to the attention of some few young, or youthful, men and women. These youths must have a persevering Will to hear and hold my propagations. It is not possible to comb the necropolises for Argonauts. I can but hope that in today's funeral procession there are proud and noble souls of any land who have Will to act.

There could be millions to escape the bombs. I speak not of the agricultural classes of the less technicalized societies, for these serfs will have been magnetized into the distended belly of the hive cities decades before the avalanche of flame. A half century is held back before hell incarnate is on earth. To a few there may be a retreat, if today they find Will to walk away from the city to go to the sheltered slope and river side. If in this instant but thousands assent to my interpretations, then by the eve of the bombings there can be millions on those plateaus furthest from the urban belts.

There must be concerted Will to bring these sanctuaries into being, none shall exist except as products of supreme dedication and labour. I plead not the cause of Walden Pond. I defend not withdrawal from duty but rather a pioneering declaration of faith in tomorrow.

To flee the fields deformed with the carcasses of a dying herd is never cowardliness. And if there is not a transcending love, concealed or apparent, then it is nonsense to be a survivor. There is not a need of your martyrdom if there is only a nonexistent future to comment on it. The hive cities are to be eliminated from the planet. A denial of life thuds at the casements of the European Age. And purges are of the Occident.

What of the young, shall they too be fumed into ash?

Death shall blot those puddles where toy boats veer steeply to drink unto their play sails the murky water. The oceans bulged with life shall be but sewers for the falling ash.

Why do I page this madness of mournful pain? Does it predict an unnatural urge to swallow fame and attention as the child who orally hungers for all he sees?

Perhaps the father of these lines is a victim of psychogenic illness. A bursting blood cell in an acute channel of the brain may have maimed this man who writes of incalculable horror. It may be said of him that in his meanderings he inculcates a misbegotten wish for death in honest folk. And then, who is this Hebrew trickster who alleges an ignition of the world's Romes? Isaac, Abraham, they were elders who replenished the wells of mankind's hope but this dangerous devil relates of a stone bridge flung to river's bottom.

He must be a Judas.

Can it be otherwise that he is not an incoherent, foulmouthed, lowly heretic?

A son of palpable malfortune affixed to his other defects seals the verdict. Alone a reason to score his enmity to this difficult but not unrewarding day. The author's remorseful persuasion of life has undoubtedly diminished this capacity for a positive opinion of this best of all possible worlds. Fellow reader, behold this resentful wretch of a once subservient race and hold him not answerable to his idiot's utterances. Instead show him Christian mercy for his soul is clearly pierced.

Undeterred I implore thee that I am responsible for my words and that my spirit is unquenchable in its inviolability to fate's imponderables.

It is because of the sadness intrinsic to the Jew, and more, that I am a child of the moment's disaster, that I have sought and found beauteous inspiration in every dawn.

Throughout this essay I have affirmed my love of life and again I shall nail this faith to page. Forever that I live I shall to myself be a Joseph, a provider of food against the coming famine. I speak not to make afraid the children of the world. And if my vision is of a terrible blaze destroying innocents, then also it is a lash that sets me to try and rework tomorrow's history. If naught is attempted the earth shall swoon in the torment of the West's fatality.

Above this planet there is not an intelligence that plots the future. Earthly time is ancient and belongs not to the spring. Earth's time is the elephant who at last ignores his mother's umbilical trunk but then eludes not the showering petals of death. So time becomes separable from her beginnings and voyages to an ending. Time of this earth shall not re-fertilize itself, time too becomes aged. All is a single leaf in a forest of actuality. Do not fear because the totality of earth is mortal. Billowing universes are prepared in a multiplication of simultaneous and diverse time funnels. There will never be end to living spores that breed. Matter, space, time, and motion are re-issuable. Yet even if the aftermath of death is life, still weep profusely for the embracing child that is no more. It is if the rivers turned to muck, it is a scarifying cataclysm if the children are destroyed, it is inconsolable sadness.

But if thee has a Will in the wellings of your person perhaps some children may be saved. Will is our lone machine for only the power of Will can resist the bombs. Shall we not compel our weakness to contest havoc's despair? Let you and I twine a slender rope to sway from this winter high above the bombs to greet the wetness of a welcoming spring. Will is of the soul and of the animal, it is mankind. Can not you sense the swelling of your hope in a revelation if you but begin this voyage.

A successful attack on the prevailing historical probabilities is not wholly impossible. Objectives must be chosen that are not exorbitant and thus only a jester's pattering. Frustration is of life. One must love not for the good happenstance but instead love because of a transcending concept of pride, of beauty, and of the Lord that reduces fear to inexperience. Love shall never desert man if he is aware of the excitement due each birth. This season must not just be tolerated. We have to combat it with our Will coerced into a reprinting of the become. Man may only change the past by structuring his present's threats. If he is able to accomplish this, then the future becomes extension.

Suddenly the instants of awareness are splintered as time is reality. Far too soon the wren slips from her snow invaded tree. The animal who forsakes guiltless purity, learning that his name is a facsimile of face, then becomes bankrupt of birth. If man conforms to disaster then it must be done. Yet if he will drink the sea, then it shall be emptied of salt.

Book VII

STILL IS THE SEA

Chapter 1

AT THE TIDE'S STATEMENT I shall see the sea anoint the land with ruthless punishment. The beach's whitened grains turn subtly pink as the sun's bleaching light passes through my body. Hearing the vaulting sea bird mount a peal of recognition as it glides in steep circles above my head, I see now that the bird holds a still minnow in her claws.

I am not sure but I believe that I may have touched the fringe of God's robe and heard Him speak through my fingers into my mind asleep yet not. He spoke and said to be afraid and not content with this world of mine now. A tear swallowed my inner life as He said this and I know not where it came from. His name is Lord and He is life and tenderness. There are no limits to the Lord's all inclusive nature. He imbues each instant with His awareness. He is not the falling limb of a storm ridden oak. He is the creator of life. The Lord is not capable of dying as He is the past, present, and future. He is the alabaster whale charging the wooden vessel of man's arrogant assumption of immortality. God's hidden name is truth. It is His love of life that is the salvation of man, but it comes only to the living and not the dead.

A new spring is desired by those who can be refreshed by living as it is. A proud morning is awaited by those who have been wounded because of their nobility of manner. A blessing Culture grows in yet this moment and pathways shall be cut past the shrubbery that protects the pristine woods. Soundings of axe and saw shall be heard across the roused land. All is not lost, the forbidden is still attainable. Man is neither meek nor congenial and in that he still is a creator.

Earth lives and man will bring forth an impressive Culture. A sense of vigorous performance that will be without falsified bravado shall gladden man's journey as time. If tomorrow there be hideous infliction, thereafter a sweeter intimacy will ensue to ease the pain. Striding kings shall adventure begin and life will not be meaningless. In the time of this final Culture a gossamer of purpose shall unite with the new spirit.

As there are seasons to the planet, the universe, and Cultures, so there is an organic measurement possible to the race of man. Each of the Cultures braid themselves into the entire story of mankind. Cultures are the notes, the emotional movements of the symphony that is the log of manor earth. There is not a progressive tale to man. Not linear descent or ascent to history, rather there are climaxes of life as conquest. Simply then, there exists a morphology of man bespeaking birth, growth, and death. Yes, in the river of experience that is man's march traversing the reality of existence, there are seasons. Man does not age biologically but he does accumulate reflexes that tend to take on characteristics of innate behavior. Man acquired a soul as his need of love was intensified by his warring against environment. And there is no surety that reality will fulfil any of his dreams.

There are seasons to the tale of mankind as a species. First there was a pre-become. Sameness of stimuli and reaction did not change until man's concept of himself and of his God prepared so slowly the original beginning spring. The six Cultures of man exist in a modified sequence of time. Their placement in a five to six thousand yeared episode clearly delineated the tens of thousands of centuries of the provisioning become that preceded it. The centering of four of the Cultures in lands adjoining the eastward basin of the Mediterranean is not causally explainable by geography or climatic conditions. There are areas on the planet where available resources surpass the mideast. Certainly the Mississippi delta is a readily attainable wealth when compared to the laborious and exact irrigations called for in the Mesopotamian valleys. The era beginning with the Nile-Euphrates Culture and ending with the West represents the short but honeyed summer of man's history.

The coming World Culture shall be the final couplet to

the poet's lines and autumn will reside in the souls and veins of men. It shall be a season of bringing in, of respite for the Gods who have patroned since the march began. We have had our spring and summer fronds and now the future is of orange rusted laminas tumbling in the evening's zephyrs. Then contiguous shall be winter, which will be the perusing of all that was, a refingering of completed creativity. The sun of winter in this case shall be of lengthy duration.

To gambol with the nymph near the high willows, to entrap her by the roots is of animal as beauty. The blood that arteries geyserlike in warfare is indistinguishable from the fluid that invigorates the lover's passion or renews the artist's mind as he contemplates himself for creation's thrust. But at last the soul shall rid man of his aggressive propensities and the ship will be hawsered and spliced to the earth.

Mankind's autumn Culture will be of warm hearth odors. Autumn will be a Culture, not an empire. Not a corpulent apparatus of bureaucratic orthodoxy but a stock of one man. One people shall be extant and they will have one name, one destiny. They will be of earth, men of earth. No other appellation shall be obligatory in expressing their location in time and history.

Man is not a sliver of bone lost amidst the granite chips. There is a man besides the angry ape, besides the marauding pillager of grace and above the mindlessness of civilized affectation. For in man there is a core of spontaneous creativity and as such the march shall not be finished on the smoldering riverside that is to be Londontown. There will be freshly notched lumber to begin the fledgling cities. A novus man will endow original Gods, art, and thought. The forces of soul, spirit, and animal will resound in the liberality of man's new world. A single language shall arise from the castoff francas of the West. This man anew shall be the sibling of the abundant rivers. Man shall persist though there be the fire storms, but not all of man. Some peoples will seed no more. A stream or two, great and minor, shall be blocked to eternity. And some fine poetry shall never know ink.

Come with me to this world re-created. It shall be not fanciful in surface appearances but will diverge from all that came before in the spirit of art and thought. It should make thee weep to know that rock shall again be molded into amazing form by an absolving power. From the coves and gorges of earth man shall come forth. He will not be leafless as he was at his first assumption for he will be attired in raiments chosen from the deposits of history's become. All that was once fact and technique will be his. He will elevate his head and sing of his brotherhood to the seas and sky.

Yet without deception this idea must be raked from my denseness. Man may not exist as man past the bombings unless he is aware that there can be a birth majestic in hope of love and not the ending flames. Hear me friends, surrender never to the diminution that the Lord cares not. Free your soul and your sons shall be replenished. I lecture not to have faith in faith, not in religious practices and observances of the past as they have been diminished to the countenance of evil. God does suffer with our pain. He is distressed at our plight but He is powerless to instruct His might. If the Lord intercedes with man we are no longer man but instead sheep that graze on pasturage. We must be stubborn with our dignity for to give up our interior freedom would mutilate that which is man.

God in linking time and motion begat matter. He authorized reality and now we are what our Will's determination makes us. We are a result not of God's wants but of His creation's need of man. From the remote clay nodules the Lord permitted time to be cognizant of space. It was from a nothingness that he addressed time and before this only He existed. He caused time to flow and from this rib of totality He gave matter to be of essence. And then this was the Lord's work, for now there was an eternity of rudiments from whence man. It was not ordained or premeditated, nor Willed by fate's chance that mankind is a fact. Man was grafted to totality because a maturing life of earth demanded it. Life Wills life and man lives. As a physical actuality man is indistinguishable but in his ascertainment of God and his contributions of art and Cultures he mates beauty regal to existence.

There shall be light for the children of man if we of this

today proudly begin the march anew. I exhort you to flee the cities and stamp your steps into the harrows. Flee the doomed cities, flee the necropolis and walk the land, ploughing and seeding the turned over soil. Come with not terror as your spur, come with hope's love. Go to those places where the bombs will not defecate on a lonely farm. Hide not your purpose but say aloud the dream so that thy neighbor may be advised of the warning. It is not a coward's action to flee the cities, though the greater portion of man shall revile you for your initiative. Hate shall be shown you by the leaders of the endangered world. Their winter skills in the manipulation of word shall be boasted at you in outrageous admonishment. Yet be reassured for among the powerful there will be those who shall offer respite.

Speak not in priestly fashion to your brothers. Utter no prophecy or incantation and dare not to say that the Lord is your benefactor and protector. Those who leave the cities are not superior to the mass who choose to stay. Remember that your father's resting place is defenseless to the burning. Expect no treasure from the earth for thy efforts. The land shall be hostile and she will think you to be a pretender.

Leave the cities not in confusion but go in compact, preequipped groups. Permit the members to be of any trade; butchers, students, soldiers, or priests. It is unimportant what your comrade's factual employment may have been for the urgency is the aspect of the inner self. A blacksmith is indispensable and thus a member must be trained in the working of iron before the exit is confirmed. Provision your needs in the cities and not ruinously strive for their fruition on the raw soil. Carry surplus bushels of seed, both solicit and purchase tools and land. Plant that which will feed twice your numbers for after the bombings throngs shall decamp from the torched cities. The majority will die of the poisoned air and water before they have traveled the heartless miles. But a few sick and healthy shall reach your haven and they will be fed. If they arrive as mobs to steal your preparedness slay them if you must. However if they beg at the doors as mendicants, as lepers, feed and treat their wants and make them welcome in all ways.

Chapter 2

ENTRUST YOUR FUTURES far from the necropolises. Seek the pools and creeks in the vacant lands of the southern continents. Shun Asia, go not to Europe for nowhere in these parts may a refuge be found. North America will be scoriae, deceive yourselves not that there is a mountain fastness that can shelter thee on that continent. Go not to the islands of the Mediterranean or Caribbean seas. Flee only to those lands despised because of their meager profitability and of their great distances from the pleasure products of the city. Fear Australia but those islands individual and chain lying eastward may remain habitable.

The interior of South America offers best escape from the corrosive dust of the inferno. I advise journey to the plateaus, the lower mountain ranges, and those unexplored streams of central and westernly parts of Iberian America. Away from the urbanized coast, go inland to celebrate the future with life. The civilized epidermis of the ocean fronted lands shall be but sporadically bombed and in the midlands there are as yet no hive cities to attract the missiles.

Africa south of the Moor's lands has relatively few ports and the rivers are fraught with obstacles. Her central area to a slighter degree than South America has been left to indigenous tribal commerce and some development of mineral reserves. However it is with trepidation that I suggest Africa for in the chapters ahead she may well place herself into a technological tomb. For Africa has decided to be pseudo aggressive, progressive, and modern. Thusly she fraternizes with this maddening season.

What does it mean to know reality only as a rain cloud that overflows itself above a city in pain? How is it to be a drop of wet that sparks into molecules of hot ether on contact with the boiling pavement?

And then what is it to know that youngsters romp where the thistledowns are not spheres of fire?

Fear not the dying of the West except as to the nature of the ending. The World Culture shall be clustered with fair life. This last commutation of creative man shall birth a poem of unpretentious glory. Kings shall be oiled and the Lord will have a newer religion to praise him. Do not weep to see the old fall down, rather feel the passion of the beginning spring.

If this promise of a becoming World Culture fails to occur, then man is condemned as a dominant species of animal. Should there not be a new Culture then man is a victim. I perceive no adhesive in the Western winter that might paste this present's decay into a reinforced civilization. The redirection of Western history using the tools of cynicism and fatuous technology seems improbable. A discipline long debilitated would be indispensable before the least of starts could be dared. The quality of Will needed for such an effort can not be manufactured by any technique or by psychological reduction.

Brave are those who refuse to surrender tomorrow to the bombs. The thought of such monstrosity but stimulates them to counter the disintegration. These men of courage strain to hold the West back from the ominous cavity. And thus they must consider my words only as the defeatism of a non-person. But by their unwillingness to be cognizant of the approaching bombs, they increase the likeliness of the fire storms. Even today's chosen champions are fevered with the agony of aberrating vision.

A coterie of intelligent men from scholastic and professional background have endeavored to resuscitate the collapsing West. Confusion is the result of their honest intentions. They falsely predicate all on the empty assumption that the ages of man are indifferent in gradations of spirit, sureness, hope, and suffering. To think that man's world is a prime number that may be dealt with as a constant factor negates logic. Reptilian man adapts to his surroundings, converting color and judgments indiscriminately. However in this age of ever increasing frustrations, he reacts by withdrawing into hapless passivity or with psychopathic instability. Winter man is an intemperate and nervous dragon.

One wick remains above the hollow of hot wax that spells extinction of the wavering light. A pragmatic world association which would introduce appeals for logic and control might restrict nuclear weaponry. In candor there is little hope that the martial and masochistic nations of this raving season could weld such a mundane organization devoted to simple survival. Alas, unless some type of voluntary association comes to fact, there shall be nothing left to be governed. Idealistic demands for the complexity of a world federation have no relevancy in a world contorted with jealousy and fear. What might be practical is an unencumbered arrangement whereby associated states would merge monetary systems, nullify all trade hindrances, and contribute to an armed force that would be superior to any single national army. Such an unsophisticated and pious plan as this might inhibit the enactment of the fire storms. Unfortunately it is foreseeable that those nations benefiting most by such arrangements will repudiate those very obligations that could offer a degree of safety.

But all attempts to unify the nations of the winter world are most probably the dreams of a narcotic. They are as laws that imply lofty principle and sentiment but become dulled tools when the spirit is lacking. Prosaic remedies besides being obvious are also in many cases the most effective. A gigantic political compromise between Russia and the United States would offer the world a wholesome opportunity for stability and sanity. These two Romes of the West's winter would have to broach an agreement ranking in clarity and purpose to appeals for a generous and forgiving brotherhood of man. A simplicity offered as when Solomon suggests to divide the disputed child asunder excepting that this contentious world would have to be doled out in two parts to the Romes if there is to be peace. Yet they both are infants to wisdom and these small hopes are but mutterings to those concerned with constructing the rocket bombs.

In this cruel moment there are men who are not deluded by the praises of the manipulators. Men with faith in the institutions and spirit of the West. They do not genuflect or dissemble but boldly swim the whirlpools of this treacherous age. If these fellows could take hold the broken rudder and tie it fast, a safe course might be set. First they themselves must accept that the effectualization of a Cultural resurrection is not possible. To wage a battle to rescue more than the ossified structure of the dying West from a catatonic stupor is absurd. Returnings of the creative floods are not possible for nothing is left in the cornucopia. All that might be salvaged from the fire's carbonization is form's fact and the lives of a huge flock. Unlikely it is but in the corners of imagination there is a flicker of hope that the West, by the application of tremendous Will, could maintain a civilization for some centuries. A World Culture still would come to pass though the West erects a sterile civilization. How good it would be if the storms of fire were forever locked away in a misplaced Pandora's box. But in this sorrowing season the proud and the noble are ostracized, leaving hopelessness to those who struggle to avoid thermonuclear war. Heroic are these few for they limit fear in man by their tightly pinioned faith. In today's quicksand it is difficult to be messenger of good will for the disgruntled mob tends to spew up those of the most disciplined of fealty.

Good men of holy training have been ensnared by a cloying socialism that is neither evil nor pernicious but does lack direction, creation, and suffers not to love God. The comparison between the early Church's reluctance to encourage money and its devotion to poverty and to this Western technical socialism is inappropriate to historical survey. Humanism is of justice and brotherhood, and in those aspects of socialism which are motivated by charity and humanity an unmaligned desire to ameliorate barbarism is observed.

Those instilled with a sense of duty to their brothers have in increasing numbers entered into the behavioral and social studies. Unhappy is my task to bespeak that this dedication to the reduction of the inward illnesses by the process of therapeutic illumination and tender concern is a symptom of winter's convolutions. History's modern disarray has tocsined the psychical adjuster into being. For without the pronounced decline of the Culture by the late nineteenth century, the alarm would have been far less severe. Emotional and mental derangement had been dispersed in such a contagious manner it predicted the need of psychological medication. The ego centered Western ethos presupposed injury of the soul when the Culture became enfeebled. Intrinsic to these humanistic skills is the erroneous denial of creativity and aggression, except as statistical normalities, in an effort to rid the individual of self-inflicted failure in an overwhelming closure of history.

Can it be that prophets wedded to God re-discovered will appear to teach self-denial and love? Shall there be those who impress man with their favor and convictions? If beings of transcendental hope should lead man to the aspiring of awareness, would they not become victims of the age's cynicism and spiritual fatigue. Indubitably they eventually would have to accept esoteric syncretism and infantile costuming in order to cajole their impatient followers. Yet to be a true prophet one must penetrate roadways clogged with barbs of withdrawal, jealousy, insatiable destruction, sadism, self-crucification, and of flagrant gratifications. His only purpose of being would be to defeat excessive fear and hate. In this mooing of mediocrity there is a pleading need of even the tiniest of prophets. A shepherd to slip from out the darkness and flare the night away so that the flocks see where unto follow. If from the sophistry of this collapsing epoch came one whose soul was refreshed by awareness, who preached of a trustful redemption, then there might be a grander hope. Where could a man as this find peace needed to ponder the remedial love unless he contorted his head to the sky and permitted the sun to burn away his memories. In the coming decades false prophets and pretense messiahs will blurt forth with incautious mystery, thus neutralizing an honest singer in his attempt to inspire the dwellers of the necropolis into recognition of their souls and destinies.

Whatever doth come, it shall not thwart the emergence of

the beginning spring. Neither bombs nor civilization shall castrate the new Culture. Clarions will call man to testify to the grandeur and joy of the young Culture. Once again man shall exert himself into happy growth. And man shall love man for his power of creation. An image newly coined shall enter into the dawning smoke as energy is remembered. Adventure will flaunt its confidence and man shall know that indomitable Will is the creator of Cultures. To wrought a Culture is not the work of cowards. It is the art of men who worship not technology but hear, as from a sea pausing reef, music that carries a far distance.

Chapter 3

THIS BOOK IS DEDICATED to all the youth of the world. If thee has the spirit to build anew, then thou has the vigorous sureness of the Bellinis, of Dante, and of Beethoven. Never doubt that there shall be a pageant of creation to sequel the bomb's thick cape of ash and dust. I enjoin you in tones of compassionate brotherhood to flee the cancerous overgrowths that our cities have become. The cities seep into each other to form a congealed morass. The grotesque city is an indication of the infection and not cause.

Childlike are those of good feeling who prognosticate favorable changes through the applications of education and time. Using the lowliest delusion to guard their own forebodings they view all ages as interchangeable in circumstance and say that evil is correctable by the fleeting moment.

My bidding is the liquid iron of the realist and is exclaimed with swiftness of word. Flee the cities, flee the nations corrupted by technology as God. Start anew, begin once again where early man lost his obsequious diffidence. Envision the miracle of the plant heavy with fruit as its winter roots are bathed in the rains and floods of yes, the awakened spring. Flee the necropolises of this soon to be capsized world. Return to the land, to the earth that shall not refuse you nourishment. Return to the harvests of grain, labour with contentment as in the blessed days of summer. Replenish your inner being with the surety of the land's offerings. Expect not a tower to be your home, instead roof a simple house to the fiery sky. Find in the charm of your wife respite from the pain of charging farm land from jungle tract and mountain side. You and your woman shall live as an adventure with ample reason to create life.

Carry in your packs and wagons books. You must bring

books to the unspoiled land for they are bulbs that bloom season upon season. Bring those vessels of printed word that illustrate man's genuine and serious efforts in art and science. Carry those volumes that paint so patently the tragedy and exhilaration of man's voyage.

Finite insight concludes that to race with death is degradation. Efficient machines do speed distances less but in doing so they also frustrate time as a horizon that man needs as his goal. Suffocated is the impulse to gift art except in those rare individuals competent of inspiration founded in their own acts of life. At this finality's close the dreams, the momentum, of the West has ceased and only the tides have motion as they take back the dead forms of what was once heroic. Europe has forgotten boldness and now resists conflict and dichotomy, the very bones of her ambition. Man has surrendered to hypnotic dependence on technology and in this very today must be sentenced for this denial of self and soul. Imbibing intoxicants that enlarge organs and skeleton has caused asphyxiation of the inner being. Yet in the truly hopeful man there resides courage to depict reality as a condition of existence that may be modulated with Will.

Grief and sorrow are the vapors of the mourner, and as history is revealed, so the denizens of the cement hives shall behold a moment hideous. In those scorching days ahead an irrevocable defeat shall unmask this season's fragility. As termination approaches man will banish achievement, potential, and pride to wallow in indulgences that were considered base abominations of better ages.

Flee the doomed cities and with your hands mortar a beginning world. Do not fear that which inhibits the voyage but go to the earth awaiting you. Goodly land is available by the virgin water that will convey your coming. Be not angered by the disparagement of those who join not the endeavor for they still are of man and thus worthy of God's love. The Machiavellians shall clang that you are cowards and prevaricators. But I say that you shall signature a mural of poetry and nobility with your Will as stroking brush. Say aloud that the sea has stilled and become a pallbearer. Yet life shall disregard the flames. Come with your friends and promulgate a new spring. I promise only harsh labour but that will reward you with tranquillity and enthusiasm. Know that with the fewest of companions thee have saved the species of life self-named man. Your sons shall proceed to the joy of composing a song of destiny. Be not timid but bind your hands together and thee shall discover an undertaking needful of courage and an endless river lovely with challenge.

The West's narrative has not an epilogue. She is disastrously enfiladed. The West is lost, history has played her stagecraft leaving the heroine with but a burning mansion.

European man loved his world greatly. From his soul's freedom he produced a cavalcade of God and king absolute in breadth of vision. A Culture in the summer of her journey lifts her peoples, institutions, and art to impossible peaks. Through art the full unveiling of her spirit is transcribed into actuality. Men of the summer presume an inviolability for they believe that their world is immortal and unconquerable.

Remember who and where you were as a child, walk barefoot on the shell strewn shores of yesterday. Forget not all you have been and restore to this moment those instants of awareness that have drifted into the descending past. Hurriedly the hours of reality break away from the present, so that it appears that this now never was. Hurl your mind back to the start, to your become. Flavor life with intuition. Be alert to the evil that pervades your moment. Be silent in your search for understanding. Hold fast to the truthful man who forbids sophism. Read history with inward vision and know that change of form and condition is normality. And if you sense history as I do, then my words shall not seem as a withdrawal from responsibility, but as a plea for refuge in a notorious age. With each particle of my nature I author this story with impassioned belief in love and creativity orchestrated by Will. I insist that man shall not die, that God is the essence of essence, and that inspired art has a substance surpassing the strength of nickeled steel.

Return to the land, flee the concrete tombs for the gates have been locked. Walk to a new spring. Love man, love his dignity though cowering with humiliation. Take my path and go to those parts where a becoming shall find man healthy and free. Be not foolish, be aware that a spring is the glory of life. Be not persecuted by the machine. Be aware that there is a power unequalled by the exploded atom. A determination toward the creation of love and meaningful symbols is a power greater than all of this world's chemicals. Trust not your hope to the gratifications of an age grown hysterical with obscenities. Begin anew with the earth as your workshop. Rekindle the campfires of the marching peoples of earth. Be the Dorics, the Arabs, and the Franks. Be the adventure itself, make your life the march of man.

Walk with me to the marshes and meadows where we shall sculpture new beginnings. Awake! Awake from the morose prisons of the injured soul. Men must assert their Wills to accomplish escape. Love man and respect him, though he lacks objectivity in all matters, trivial and great. He has not prevision but to some there is a beholding of indistinct images.

This moment is not similar to past happenings, it is unique to World History and demands unique wisdom to overcome its destructive bent. There were ages richer in spirit, if poorer in life span and material well-being. And moments lost with profusions of art and thought. The homeless of this winter may acquire wealth but they waste their honour in the attainment of self-flagellation.

There is no one to save the race of man except you. How might I scribe the becoming spring to entice you away from the common grave. There is little time remaining, those that desire to continue the voyage should make their decisions now. Bells will not boast that you begin adventure, for abuse, not garlands shall be showered on you as thee leave the cities. Be not deterred by the material wealth of the billions who remain for a destructive insanity is poised voraciously beneath the wailing sheets of success.

Some men are born to raise the masts of Viking ships and some to slavery as emasculated souls. Many die young and but a few old, yet all are born into life and that must be enough to sustain each through his journey. The workings of man in the poorest household are wondrous for there are children to be loved and joy to be hoped in their futures. Fewest are those who bear visions. A society of angry apes best rears prophets, thus winter may bud the rarest of fruits. Be of those few who guide man to change history's fall. Advance from the necropolises to the slumbering land, fear not that you forfeit for the fairest graces are far from the city hutches.

Blessed are those who love themselves as they wish to love their brothers. Be not ashamed of desiring to live in the future by your seed. Be not guilty for daring to begin anew as the creators of the last Culture of man. Be not afraid to choose yourself to sail a great adventure. Be proud of your pride's courage for it marks you a son of the Western Age.